WITHDRAWN

HARVARD LIBRARY

WITHDRAWN

# MODERN GREEK PHILOSOPHERS ON THE HUMAN SOUL

Selections from the writings of Five Representative Thinkers of Modern Greece on the Nature and Immortality of the Soul, translated and edited with a Preface, Introduction, and Notes

By

CONSTANTINE CAVARNOS

INSTITUTE FOR BYZANTINE
AND MODERN GREEK STUDIES
115 Gilbert Road
Belmont, Massachusetts

All rights reserved
Copyright, 1967, by Constantine Cavarnos
Published by THE INSTITUTE FOR BYZANTINE AND
MODERN GREEK STUDIES
115 Gilbert Road, Belmont, Massachusetts 02178
Printed in the United States of America

## PREFACE

The purpose of this book is twofold. It is intended, in the first place, to focus attention on what is, to my mind, the most vital theme for man, that of his soul, its nature and immortality. This subject is very sadly neglected today, not only by philosophers, but also by theologians. There is great need, therefore, for works that stimulate and enlighten men's thoughts regarding it. This book intended also to acquaint the English speaking world better with modern Greek philosophic thought, about which extremely little is known outside of Greece.

I have selected from the works of five representative modern Greek thinkers — Benjamin, Vrailas-Armenis, Skaltsounis, St. Nectarios, and Theodorakopoulos — chapters or sections that deal with the question of the nature of the human soul and its immortality, and have translated them from the original Greek as accurately as possible. The works from which these selections have been taken date from 1820 to 1949. I have added occasional footnotes, in order to clarify certain terms or points in the texts, or to show the closeness of the teaching contained in them to that of well-known philosophers and scientists of other times or lands. Moreover, as the life of a distinguished author is always of special interest and helps one see his thought in the proper perspective, I have inserted a biographical note on each of the five Greek philosophers at the beginning of the sections containing their texts.

For those who may wish to pursue further the study of modern Greek philosophic thought on this topic, I have added a bibliography at the end of the book, under the heading of "Further Reading."

In translating modern Greek proper names I have followed the phonetics of the modern Greek language. But in transliterating other Greek words I have used the system commonly employed by English scholars.

Part of the research required for the preparation of this work was done during the academic years 1957-58 and 1958-59, when, as a Fulbright Research Scholar affiliated with the University of Athens, I did research in the field of modern Greek thought.

I must express here my deepest gratitude to the United States Government for having made possible for me research in that field for two years. I must also thank Professor George B. Burch of Tufts University and Dr. Arthur Nikelly of the University of Illinois, for kindly reading the entire manuscript and making many valuable suggestions.

CONSTANTINE CAVARNOS

*Clark University*
*Worcester, Massachusetts*
*September,* 1967

# CONTENTS

|  | Page |
|---|---|
| Preface | 3 |
| Introduction | 7 |

### I. BENJAMIN (1762-1824)
| | |
|---|---|
| Biographical Note | 15 |
| 1. Existence of the Soul as a Spiritual Substance | 17 |
| 2. Freedom of the Soul | 20 |
| 3. Immortality of the Soul | 22 |

### II. VRAILAS-ARMENIS (1812-1884)
| | |
|---|---|
| Biographical Note | 31 |
| 1. On the Nature of the Soul | 33 |
| 2. Science and the Soul | 37 |

### III. SKALTSOUNIS (1824-1905)
| | |
|---|---|
| Biographical Note | 43 |
| 1. Criticism of Materialism | 45 |
| 2. Spiritual Nature of the Soul | 50 |
| 3. Immortality of the Soul | 53 |

### IV. ST. NECTARIOS (1846-1920)
| | |
|---|---|
| Biographical Note | 57 |
| 1. Prolegomena | 59 |
| 2. Proofs of the Soul's Immortality | 61 |

### V. THEODORAKOPOULOS (1900 —)
| | |
|---|---|
| Biographical Note | 89 |
| Concerning the Soul | 91 |

| | |
|---|---|
| Further Reading | 106 |
| Index | 109 |

## ILLUSTRATIONS

|  | Page |
|---|---|
| Petros Vrailas-Armenis | 30 |
| Ioannis Skaltsounis | 42 |
| St. Nectarios Kephalas | 56 |
| Ioannis Theodorakopoulos | 88 |

# INTRODUCTION

In the first systematic treatise on the soul, that written by Aristotle more than two thousand years ago, the great dignity and value of knowledge of the soul is stressed. At the opening of that work, entitled *Peri Psychēs,* "On the Soul," Aristotle remarks: "We regard all knowledge as beautiful and precious, but one kind of it more so than another, either by reason of its exactness or because it has reference to superior or more wonderful objects. On both these counts it is reasonable to place the study of the soul among subjects of the foremost rank."

The great importance of this knowledge springs from the nature of the soul itself, which Aristotle learned to value from his teacher Plato, who in turn had learned to esteem it from his master Socrates. The latter identified man with the soul, and exhorted his fellow Athenians to direct their efforts above all to its improvement. In the *Apology* written by Plato, Socrates tells the Athenians: "I do nothing but go about persuading you all, old and young alike, to take thought neither of your bodies nor of your properties, before you have given the utmost care to the greatest improvement of your souls."[1] The soul, Socrates held, is essentially independent of the body and immortal; and hence time and effort expended in improving it are most prudently spent; for "inasmuch as the soul is manifestly immortal, there is no release or salvation from evil except the attainment of the highest virtue and wisdom."[2]

---

[1] 30a-b.
[2] *Phaedo,* 107c-d

Prior to him, Pythagoras, Heraclitus, Empedocles, and other Greek philosophers had laid similar stress on the reality and dignity of the human soul, and the need for improving or "purifying" it.

With regard to Aristotle, it might be objected that his view of the soul is rather different from that of Plato, Socrates, and the other philosophers I have mentioned; and that the high dignity he attributes to it at the beginning of his treatise *On the Soul* is not at all consonant with the conception of it which he advances in Bk. II, Ch. 1. Here he defines the soul as "the actuality (*entelecheia*) of a natural body potentially possessing life,"[3] and goes on to say that the soul, so defined, is not separable from the body. From this it follows that the soul perishes when the body dies — is not immortal, as it is for Socrates, Plato, and the others. But it should be noted that here Aristotle is speaking of psyche in general, whether found in plants or animals; and that when he turns to the human psyche, in the next book, he asserts that the higher part of the soul, *nous* or reason, which distinguishes man from the beasts, is separable from the body and hence immortal.[4] In another work, *On the Generation of Animals,* he says that the rational soul "comes from outside" (*thyrathen*), and enters the body at the time of conception.[5] Further, in the *Nichomachean Ethics,* Aristotle exhorts us not to listen to the materialists: "We must not follow those who enjoin us, being men, to think of human things, and being mortal of mortal things, but we ought, so far as possible, to make ourselves immortal, and do all that we can to live in accordance with the best thing in us — *nous*; for . . . in power and value it far surpasses everything else. And it may be held that this is each man's true self, inasmuch as it is the chief and better part of him."[6]

When the Greeks were Christianized, when the pagan Greek world was replaced by the Christian world of Byzantium, they assimilated into Christian teaching many elements from Greek philosophy, which, as Clement of Alexandria says in his *Strom-*

---

[3] 412a19 ff.
[4] III, Chs. 4-5. Cf. *Meta.,* XII, 3, 1070a25-28.
[5] 737a5.
[6] X, 7, 1177b33-1178a3.

*ateis,* "was a schoolteacher to bring the Hellenic mind, as the Law the Hebrews, to Christ.[7] Among these elements were many from the psychology of Plato. The Greeks of Byzantium discarded Plato's ideas of the preexistence, reincarnation and transmigration of the human soul, but upheld his teaching that it is a simple, uncompounded, incorporeal, self-active, wholly imperishable substance, which acts upon the body and is acted upon by it, and possesses three main powers: the rational, the spirited, and the appetitive. Like Plato, they insistently affirmed the immortality of the human soul; and some of them, such as St. Athanasius, St. Gregory of Nyssa, and St. Maximus the Confessor, undertook to prove its immortality by rational arguments as well as by reference to Holy Scripture. The soul, they assert, does not perish when the body dies. It survives in its entirety the death of the body, as a conscious, personal being, and will experience either happiness or suffering, depending on the quality of its life on earth, until the day of the Resurrection and Judgment, when the souls will be invested with spiritual, indestructible bodies. Thereafter the soul will share with the body in unspeakable blessings (Heaven) or in unspeakable torments (Hell).

As inheritors of both the ancient Greeks and of the Byzantines, modern Greek philosophers have stressed the reality and dignity of the human soul, and have sought to prove its incorporeal nature and immortality. Further, they have subjected to criticism opposed conceptions, such as those of materialism, naturalism, and positivism. Of the ancients, their chief teacher regarding the soul has been Plato. While having much less recourse to Aristotle, they have seen in him an ally against such schools of thought, because of his emphatic affirmation of the existence of God and of the immateriality and immortality of *nous,* which he viewed as man's true self. Like the Byzantines, they have not accepted Plato's doctrines of preexistence and reincarnation, or his identification of man exclusively with the soul. Although they view man as being primarily and chiefly the soul, as Christians they regard the body as a part of human nature and believe in its resurrection.

---

[7] Bk. I, Ch. 5.

In the West, many philosophers of the last and of the present century have sought to model philosophy after the sciences, and to solve metaphysical problems, such as that of the soul, by means of the scientific method. The result has been that the soul has eluded their grasp. Characteristically, they do not speak of the soul, but only of some of its activities, such as thinking and consciousness. And their views about the nature and source of these is vague and evasive. Modern Greek thinkers, on the other hand, have viewed philosophy as a discipline that is higher than science, having its own method and qualified to be science's critic.

Moreover, in the West, the tendency has been in modern times to divorce philosophy from religion, and to philosophize quite independently of religion. The Greeks, on the other hand, have kept their philosophy in close touch with their Orthodox Christian faith. Their philosophical inquiry is guided by their religious faith, and recognizes the need of being consummated by such faith. In this respect, as in others, they are quite like the Byzantines.

There have been exceptions, men who broke with their classical and Byzantine traditions, and followed scientific materialism, which they imported from Western Europe. But they have been few, and of second or third rate importance. They do not represent the main stream of modern Greek philosophic thought.

The method to be followed by the philosopher in his attempt to know the soul is that of reason and inner observation, introspection. This is the method employed by the five philosophers whose teaching on the human soul is presented in this volume. Outer, sense-observation is of no avail here, as the soul is not something external, visible, but something internal, invisible.

Using this method, these writers conclude that the soul is an entity distinct from the body; that it is a created immaterial substance, simple, uncompounded, indivisible, self-active, self-conscious, rational, free, and hence immortal. The immortality of the soul is seen to rest ultimately on the justice, goodness, wisdom, and power of God. Benjamin of Lesvos especially stresses this, and in order to give finality to his arguments for immortality he proceeds to prove the existence of God, Who is omnipotent, all-wise, just, providential of all His creatures. Vrailas-Armenis, too, sees the close relationship between immortality and God, and hence in his book *Letters of Philotheos and Eugene,* after dealing in Part I with the question of the nature of the soul, he goes on in Part II to deal with the question of God. It is in the second part chiefly that he undertakes to prove the immortality of the soul. St. Nectarios, who has treated the problem of the immortality of the soul more extensively than any other Greek writer, either ancient, medieval, or modern, similarly sees the close connection between immortality and God; and some of his nineteen proofs of the immortality of the soul, especially the last one, which is the longest, are simultaneously proofs of the existence of God. The rest of the authors, selections from whose writings on the soul are presented in this volume — Skaltsounis and Theodorakopoulos — similarly relate the immortality of the soul to God.

The point they insist upon is that God, being all-just, all-good, all-wise, and all-powerful, would neither bring about nor tolerate the annihilation of the human soul. Such annihilation would render all striving for inner perfection utterly meaningless in the end and would contradict these Divine attributes.

In having recourse to God, these philosophers are not resorting to a mere artifice in order to solve a metaphysical difficulty. The idea of God is an organic part of the world view to which they are committed, both as philosophers employing reason and as Christians with living faith.

All the texts that follow have the impress of authenticity, of profound sincerity. Their authors do not deal with the subject of the soul as a mere academic issue, but as one which is of vital concern to them, and as one which they believe should be of similar concern to all persons. And they bring to bear a great deal of fresh thinking.

CONSTANTINE CAVARNOS

# I
# BENJAMIN OF LESVOS
(1762-1824)

## BIOGRAPHICAL NOTE ON
## BENJAMIN

Benjamin of Lesvos, who is known as a "Great Educator of the Nation," because he dedicated his life to the moral, intellectual and spiritual rebirth of Greece, was born in 1762 at Plomari, Lesvos. He studied first at the school of Kydoniai (Aivali), a city on the west coast of Asia Minor, and then at the celebrated schools in the islands of Patmos and Chios. Subsequently he went to Pisa and then to Paris, where he studied mathematics, physics, astronomy, and philosophy for a period of about nine years. His strong interest in astronomy led him to visit London, in order to see the famous Herschel telescope. Returning to Kydoniai in 1798 or 1799, he became director of the school there. He taught the mathematical and physical sciences as well as philosophy at this school until 1812. After unsuccessful attempts to establish a school in his native island, he went to Constantinople, where he stayed for a period of four to five years. In 1818, at the invitation of the ruler of Wallachia, he went to Bucharest to become head of the Academy in that city and reorganize it into a college. Two years later we find him in Smyrna, head of the Evangeliki School. When the Greek War of Independence broke out in 1821, he took an active part in it, becoming a member of the legislative body of Greece and of various national committees. He died on August 26, 1824, at Nauplion, seat of the revolutionary government and center of the struggle for freedom.

His publications comprise, besides two handbooks of mathematics, a treatise in metaphysics, entitled *Stoicheia tēs Metaphysikēs*

("Elements of Metaphysics"), which was printed in 1820 at Vienna, and an unpublished volume on ethics.

Benjamin was not a partisan of any philosophical school, although his theory of knowledge shows the influence of Aristotle and Locke, both of whom he admires. His general conception of God and of man is Christian, while his view of the soul shows the influence of Plato.

# *Benjamin of Lesvos*

## 1. EXISTENCE OF THE SOUL AS A SPIRITUAL SUBSTANCE[1]

As long as man studies and meditates on celestial and earthly things, he studies and meditates on something other than himself. When, however, from the contemplation of the bodies around him he passes to the contemplation of the soul (*psyche*), then he studies and meditates on nothing other than himself, the soul having become both the inquirer and the object of inquiry. But it seems that the acquisition of knowledge of oneself is the most difficult of human problems, and this is why there existed the divine oracle: "Know thyself."[2] And surely this is the reason why there has been such disagreement among the learned about the nature of the soul. Such a thing was not without ground. For we cannot acquire an idea of the soul directly, but only through reflection, that is, through sensations, ideas, the intellect, and the desires of the soul, which certainly are not the soul itself but effects either of external bodies or directly of the soul. And the attributes

---

1 This section and that on the "Immortality of the Soul" consist of selections from the last two chapters of *Stoicheia tes Metaphysikes,* Vienna, 1820.

2 In the temple of Apollo at Delphi there was an inscription: "Know thyself." See Plato, *Charmides,* 164d ff. and Protagoras, 343b. The difficulty of knowing the soul has been stressed by other writers, too, such as Aristotle, who remarks: "To attain any assured knowledge about the soul is one of the most difficult things in the world" (*On the Soul,* Bk. I, 402a10-11).

themselves of the soul are not apprehended otherwise than through their effects. Thus the difficulty in knowing *what the soul* or *self* (*ego*) *is* is somehow natural.

That the soul is something, nobody, I think, can doubt. For we have named soul that in us which feels, thinks, and wills. And since the unbribable judge within us, I mean consciousness, testifies that there occur in us sensations, thoughts, and volitions — that is, effects — there must necessarily exist within us the cause of these, which has been named the soul.

The soul being something — for there is its activity — it must be one of three things: a body, a property of a body, or something immaterial. Apart from these we humans neither have nor can form an idea about it.

To begin with, then, let us suppose that it is a property or power of the body. Such a view of it appears to have been held by Epicurus, Aristoxenus, Galen, and certain others. But it is universally admitted that a property or power of a body is not something self-existent, that is, a substance, but simply a certain relation of the parts of the body either to each other or to another body. . . . It is evident, however, that the soul is not of this nature. When sensations are present, one could say that there are also present other bodies in proximity to the brain, and this is why our power of sensation manifests itself; but in the activities of the intellect we have nothing but the soul. And the consciousness of each one metaphysically confirms this: that his soul thinks about the same subject both at night and in the daytime, and at every place. . . . Moreover, the soul remembers and is conscious at the same time that it, which is now feeling or thinking, is the very same one that felt, thought, or willed many years ago. Hence, the soul is not a property or power of the body, but a self-existent entity.

But if the soul is not a power of the body, much less is it a quality. For a quality is nothing else than a certain texture of the particles of a body, or a certain relationship among them. . . . Hence, to say that which remembers past events, which anticipates future ones, which examines present ones, etc. is a relationship among the particles of the body would be outright madness.

Further, if the soul were a quality, or property, or power of the body, its activities should have been of one kind, like those of other powers, or, speaking more correctly, it should have been a certain activity, and not a chameleon, as we ourselves can observe. For moving the body is essentially different from apprehending the stimuli of external bodies; and the apprehension of the stimuli of external bodies is essentially different from thinking; and thinking is essentially different from remembering past events. The fact then that there coexist simultaneously so many and still more powers in one and the same entity, the soul, means that the soul is a self-existent being; that is, a substance and not a quality or power of the body.

Now if the soul is a self-existent being, or a substance, it follows that the soul is either matter, having various powers, or is an immaterial substance. Those who hold that the soul is material would be called *materialists*. . . .

Let us suppose that the soul is a body. . . . The materialists should tell us how the direction which is once given to it changes itself into a different one, since this is impossible for bodies. Now, for instance, I think that I am walking about the school in Patmos, and suddenly I go to Constantinople; now I think of celestial things and now of earthly things, now of virtue and now of vice. In thus passing non-temporally from thought to thought, or from movement to movement, it is the same as if my soul were changing her state by itself. But what is the change of the state of something by the thing itself, except a change without an external force? Hence the soul is not a body.

Dynamics, that is, the science through which we calculate the movements of bodies, is founded on the principle that *matter is indifferent both with reference to movement and with reference to rest,* and that in order for *the smallest change of movement to occur to a body an outside force is necessary,* wherefore bodies have been called inert. . . . According to this science, if a body happens to be in movement, it will remain in movement eternally, and if at rest it will remain at rest eternally, unless a certain external force should change its state. Hence, if the soul were a body, it would necessarily be inert. But the soul is endowed with freedom; and this means that it is not inert, inasmuch it has within itself the source of its thoughts and movements. Therefore, the soul is not a body. . . .

From what has been set forth thus far,[3] it follows that the soul is not a body. Since a body is something extended, composite, inert, etc., whereas the soul has the diametrically opposite properties, that is, it is not-extended, not-composite, and not-inert, it follows that the soul must be essentially different from a body, which means that the soul is immaterial. Thus the soul is a self-existent entity, to which the name *spirit* (*pneuma*) has been given.

We conclude from all that has been said that man is constituted of two essentially different substances:[4] spirit and body. Spirit is a substance that is simple, by nature active, rational, and free, whereas body is a substance that is composite, extended, impenetrable, and inert.[5] The spirit cares for the body and governs it, while the body serves the spirit and executes its volitions. And the spirit, like another creator, constructs through the ideas within it an intelligible world similar to the sensible one, while the body, moving from place to place, fulfills the wishes of the spirit.

## 2. FREEDOM OF THE SOUL[6]

We have metaphysical certainty that we feel, that we think and that we move, and that we move with a certain feeling or idea. Moreover, we are no less certain that every feeling and every idea is nothing else than a disposition of our soul. With regard

---

[3] I have abridged considerably Benjamin's discussion on this topic.

[4] The concept of substance has been ruled out of existence by most academic philosophers of our time. But it is well to recall here a remark made by A. N. Whitehead, one of the great critics of this notion. "Substance and quality, as well as simple location," he says, "are the most natural ideas for the human mind. It is the way in which we think of things, and without these ways of thinking we could not get our ideas straight for daily use. There is no doubt about this" (*Science and the Modern World*, New York, 1925, p. 53). J. B. Pratt, a champion of the category of substance, holds that if we refuse to accept some form of substance doctrine, we must, in the end, either deny existence, or accept some form of phenomenalism (*Personal Realism*, New York, 1937, p. 72).

[5] Cf. Bergson: "Matter is inertia, geometry, necessity . . . . Consciousness is freedom" (*Mind-Energy*, New York, 1920, p. 17).

[6] Selection from Chapter 13 of *Stoicheia tes Metaphysikes*.

## Freedom of the Soul

to these movements and activities there are two possibilities: either my soul is free, or it is not; that is, the source of the movement is either within it or is outside it. . . .

If man lacked the power of free choice and self-ruling (*autexousion*), that is, if the source of his actions were external to him, why is it that he repents, that he is sorry when he does what he ought not to do? What person who has been pulled forcibly by someone repents that he has been pulled? What person who has been robbed of his clothes by brigands repents that he has been robbed? What person who has been flogged by someone repents that he has been flogged? Nobody. But if one murders one's father, or cuts one's hand, or spends one's wealth prodigally, one feels regret. Why? Because he is conscious that the contrary was within his power. Therefore, man has the power of free choice and self-ruling.

The common opinion of all men could also be taken as a proof that man is free, that is, that the source of his acts does not lie outside himself. For if the source of man's acts lay outside himself, to what end have laws been written and punishments decreed for the transgressors and rewards for the law-abiding? And what need would there have been for counsels? What need for threats or for eternal hell? Why, pray, should there have been praise and blame? How could there have been virtue and vice, if there were only compulsion? And how could it have been just to seize a murderer, if what he committed were impossible for him to avoid? How would this have differed from punishing the knife that killed the man? And what justice would there have been in crowning the tyrannicide, if he liberates his country not voluntarily, but compulsively? . . .

There is a faction that deprives man of his free will for no other reason than that God has foreknowledge. But how is what is foreknown dependent upon him who foreknows? I know very well that the negligent student will not make progress. What follows from this? That I am the cause of his ignorance or negligence? The physician often foreknows that his patient will die. Does it follow from this that the physician's foreknowledge is the cause of the patient's death, and not the latter's illness?

Similarly, then, God foreknows very well all things before they happen; but his foreknowledge is not a determination of them to happen thus or otherwise.

### 3. IMMORTALITY OF THE SOUL

Having been proved to be simple or without parts, it naturally follows that the soul is incorruptible. For actually corruption is nothing else than the dissolution of something composite into the parts or elements that constitute it. Thus, because the soul is simple, without parts, it is insusceptible of dissolution into simpler components. Hence, when it has been separated from the body there is no reason why it should not remain alive as before, preserving its own powers. This means that the soul is immortal.

"But everything that has a beginning," one might say, "must also have an end, hence the soul, too; and God alone is immortal, being beginningless." But what do we mean by death, except the cessation of the activities of a substance? Thus, we say that a man has died when he has ceased moving and breathing. But because the soul is a simple as well as an active substance, its death or the cessation of its activities could come about only through a reduction of it to complete nonbeing. For inasmuch as the soul is simple and has no parts into which to be dissolved so as to lose its properties, its death would necessarily be nothing else than its annihilation. But this is something that does not occur even in the case of bodies. In the corruption and perishing of bodies, that is, in their death, not one of their particles is lost, but after the dissolution of the body they all become parts of other bodies, then of others, and so on forever; and this means that they are never reduced to nothing. And who else can reduce things to nothing, but their Creator alone, God? Assuming, then, that a certain creature of God is to be annihilated, this can only be effected through the will of the Creator of Nature; it cannot be brought about in any other way. Hence, if the annihilation or death of the soul is to occur, this will depend on nothing else

Thus, through a consideration of the soul with a view to but the Divine will.

# Immortality of the Soul

proving its immortality, we have unexpectedly been led to the Divine will; which means to the existence of another being that also is a spirit and immortal. It is clear, however, that the immortality of the soul is essentially different from that of God. For God is essentially immortal: He has not had a beginning and will not have an end, and for that reason He is called *eternal* (*aidios*). He is dependent on nothing, whereas the immortality of the soul is in a way a half immortality, because there was a time when the soul did not exist, having received its being and nature from God Himself, and hence its life also is dependent on the will of God, and without Him it would at every moment lapse into nonbeing.[7] It remains for us to see whether God wants to lead the soul to nonbeing or death.

But God is all-wise, all-good, all-powerful, just. It is therefore impossible that He should do something unreasonably, or should not desire the happiness of some creature of His, or should not be able to bring about what He wills, or should do something unjustly . . . .[8]

There is in man, as our consciousness testifies, a desire for our happiness, a desire, however, that remains unfulfilled on earth. But since man is neither beginningless nor self-created, but has been created by God, it is evident that this desire is the work of the right hand of the Most High,[9] of his Creator. But since this desire, as every one sees, is not fulfilled on earth, it follows that there must be another realm for its fulfillment, otherwise the all-wise God endowed man with something without knowing that its fulfillment is impossible. Thus it is contrary to God's wisdom that man be mortal.

---

[7] "For in Him we live," says the Apostle, "and move and have our being" (*The Acts of the Apostles*, 17: 28). (Note by Benjamin.)

[8] A similar view has been expressed by Plato. In the *Timaeus* 41a-b, he has the Demiurge or supreme God say: "My creations are indissoluble, if so I will. All that is bound may be undone, but only an evil being would wish to undo that which is harmonious and happy. Wherefore, since you are but creatures, you are not altogether immortal and indissoluble, but you shall certainly not be dissolved, nor be liable to the fate of death, having in my will a greater and mightier bond than those with which you were bound at the time of your birth."

[9] Cf. Psalm 77: 10.

Laws are not just given to the world, otherwise legislators would be irrational. Now we see a law written by the hand of God in the heart of man, telling him to seek his happiness, which is always to be found in the path of virtue. Then we see that the virtuous man is not always happy on earth. There must, therefore, be another life, where both virtue and happiness will co-exist in the same person; otherwise the laws have been inscribed by God in vain, which is contrary to God's wisdom. Hence man is not mortal.

God creates man out of nothing; He creates him composite, made up of spirit and body; He creates him a master of his own volitions; He creates him, as every one sees, a lord of the creatures on earth; He creates him in His image and likeness, or rational. Now if man's soul were mortal, how would he differ from the beasts? In that he knows his own wretchedness? In that he sees with his own eyes his own annihilation? Thus, it is altogether foreign to Divine wisdom that man be mortal. . . .

Furthermore, there has been no race on earth that has not believed that the virtuous are rewarded and the wicked are held accountable in the other life. Arabs, Phoenicians, Persians, Assyrians, Chaldeans, Chinese, Americans, Hebrews, Greeks, and so on have believed and continue to believe in Judgment and Retribution for the deeds performed in this life. And because the voice of all mankind, a voice uninterrupted from the beginning of the world to this day, is certainly the voice of nature, the soul of man is necessarily immortal.

Why is there so much esteem and love in man for virtuous actions, even when the person who performs them is someone else? Why is there such affliction in the soul and such shame when one does shameful deeds, or such contempt and aversion when others perform them? Why is there such a severe condemnation by conscience regarding one's most secret deeds? Whence the severe censure of conscience, which no power can stop or annihilate? Did the hand of the Almighty, Who created man, write in vain with indelible letters those feelings in his heart, without a view to retribution but intending everything to come to an end in this life? Indisputably, no . . . .

## *Immortality of the Soul*

God exercises providence for His own creatures, as the permanence and order of visible things confirm. He Himself certainly created man, too; He and no one else inscribed laws in his heart that everyone can read within himself. But we see both just and unjust men on earth; that is, both men who fulfill these Divine laws and men who despise them, without the former being rewarded for their virtue and the latter being punished for their wickedness; whereas we see men on earth chastising the transgressors of their own laws and rewarding the obeyers. So there must necessarily be another realm, where virtue will be rewarded and wickedness punished; otherwise we must deprive God of all justice, and consequently conclude that *God does not exist.* For if God exists, He must necessarily be just.[10] But because He both exists and is just, the soul must be immortal.[11]

Thus, in order to prove the immortality of the soul, we have had to refer to the existence of God. But lest this be considered a begging of the question, it is necessary that we prove that God exists.

If one lifts one's eyes towards heaven, one will see in this vast space that surrounds us infinite bodies, great bodies, bodies separated from us by immense distances, bodies of different diameters, bodies that are self-luminous and bodies that are illuminated by others, bodies at rest and bodies moving with the fastest and most orderly motion . . . ; of those moving, some having the Sun as the center of their revolution and others the planets . . . and this from the foundation of the world to this day, without their motion having become in the slightest degree slower or manifested the least disorder. Thus one would be forced to admit a certain cause of all these things, to which our forefathers gave the name God (*Theos*). . . .

---

10 "He who asserts that there is nothing after this life must assert that there is no God, either. . . . For if there is nothing beyond death, then neither is there a God. For if God exists, He is just. . . . And if He is just, He gives to each what he deserves" (Chrysostom, *Concerning Providence,* IV). [Note by Benjamin.]

11 In a like vein, John Fiske, in dealing with the question of a future life, concludes: "For my own part, I believe in the immortality of the soul. . . . as a supreme act of faith in the reasonableness of God's work" (*The Destiny of Man,* Boston and New York, 1844, p. 116).

Examine each organ of the animals, and in each you will see attested the existence of God. Who, pray, can doubt that the eyes of the animals were made in order to see, their ears in order to hear, the feet in order to walk, the hands in order to grasp and hold, the wings of birds in order to fly in the air, or the fins of fish for the water, and so on? Now the works of men imply the existence of some craftsman: that is, a rational being; why, then, in the case of natural things, doesn't the idea of a final cause (or purpose) imply the idea of God? Final causality in the realm of natural things is nothing else than the voice of God to man, provided one has ears. And in this dialect the signs are natural and the interpretation innate.

Pass on to the examination of your own organs, and in each one of them you will see depicted the creative hand of God. The anatomy of the human body shows that the structure of your eye is the most wonderful work of art of an all-wise Artist. The art which nature used in the construction of your eye evokes astonishment in man. . . .

What about human reason? Is it not the most wonderful creation in this world, an indisputable sign that its Creator is rational? For whence did man, who is not beginningless, receive this power of thinking, except from his Creator? By means of this faculty man goes out to the heavens, moves from star to star, passes through the vast space itself, and concludes his movement with the affirmation of their Creator, Whom we call God. For in asserting final causality one is asserting a Rational Cause.

Descend, O man, into the inmost depths of your heart, and there you will read two laws, surely inscribed by a certain hand, so that through one of them you might be led to seek your own happiness, and through the other you might desire the same for others — which we have named virtue. But as laws are never written without the hand of a legislator — I mean of some rational being — it necessarily follows that there must exist a certain Legislator of nature, Whom we call God. . . .

Moreover, it is beyond all dispute that motion is something unessential to matter and does not originate from its nature, like inertia, extension, impenetrability, etc. Dynamics, or the science

## Immortality of the Soul

through which we calculate motion, is chiefly grounded in this: "Matter is indifferent both in relation to motion and to rest, and an external force is necessary if even the smallest change is to take place in it, either in the way of motion or of rest." Now since motion is unessential to matter, it necessarily follows that a certain external cause imparted motion to it. This cause we call God.

What about the fact that all the nations profess the existence of God? Is not this a very strong proof of the existence of God, and that the universe is not a spontaneous creation, but the creation of a rational and all-wise Being? For Parthians, Medes, Elamites, Barbarians, Greeks, Jews, Africans, Americans, Hindus, and all the rest of the nations, both ancient and modern, unanimously declare that God exists. Their voice has resounded and resounds from the remotest parts of the earth, from the beginning of the world to this day, about the existence of God. . . .[12]

Yet some have raised objections about the existence of God, those who are called *atheists*. It is difficult, however, to be convinced that a rational being could ever reach such a point of ignorance, that seeing and studying this universe he would disbelieve in the existence of God. . . .

"The human race," they say, "got the idea of God from its ignorance of natural causes, for where men are unable to understand the cause of a phenomenon they name it God." Let us assume this to be so. But if this were true, then only the ignorant should be pious, and even more so the animals, which are ignorant of all causes, and not the profound and great minds, which have discovered those causes that we know today, as for instance Pythagoras, Archimedes, Plato, Newton, Descartes, and the rest. What, has atheism reached the height of the knowledge of things and penetrated the impenetrable mysteries of nature? But who among the atheists has ever discovered a certain law of nature, or even

---

[12] After this argument, Benjamin gives a series of what he calls "metaphysical proofs" of God. These proofs, together with those given above, which are based more on experience, lead to the following final conclusion: "That there is a Being who is beginningless, absolute, necessary, incorruptible, eternal, simple, one, omnipotent, creator of all things, all-wise, just, providential of all his creatures, and in a word God." There follow replies to objections.

somewhat approached a certain mystery of nature? Actually, one must say quite the opposite, that is, unless one has sunk to extreme ignorance one will never lack this primary knowledge, the knowledge that a Mind created things.

It is also false that the idea of God was implanted in the hearts of men by fear. For while it is true that at first men were frightened by thunder, lightning, thunderbolts, eclipses, earthquakes, etc., as a great many are frightened today also, it is altogether unreasonable to hold that men arrived at the idea of God as a result of this fear. For if fear were the cause of the idea of God, then men should have discarded this idea when they discovered the causes of these phenomena. It is obvious, however, that nothing of this sort followed.

It is also false that the idea of God was implanted into the hearts of men by the deception of the priests. For the existence of a priesthood necessarily presupposes the existence of God, just as the existence of slaves presupposes the existence of masters. So that if there were priests in the world to deceive the people, as the atheists hold, this proves that there pre-existed the idea of God in the people. And just as it is nonsense, when there are no masters, to say that the slaves advise their fellow slaves to submit to their masters, so it is clearly absurd to say that there were functionaries of God when there is no God.

No less false is the view that the idea of God was invented by the rulers. For all the histories and travel accounts of the world unanimously agree that men were first worshippers of God and then, after the passage of centuries, they formed principalities and kingdoms. And it is obviously impossible for someone to act before coming into existence. Further, if the rulers succeeded in deceiving the people into believing in the existence of a nonexistent being, how could they have been able to effect this in the minds of philosophers? Who, I ask, deceived Confucius of China, Hermes and the Hierophants of Egypt, the Gymnosophists of India, Zoroaster of Persia, the Druids of the Celts, Orpheus of Thrace, Anacharsis of Scythia, Socrates of Greece, Newton of England, and all the others?

# II

# PETROS VRAILAS-ARMENIS
## (1812 - 1884)

Petros Vrailas-Armenis

# BIOGRAPHICAL NOTE ON VRAILAS-ARMENIS

Petros Vrailas-Armenis, the foremost Greek philosopher of the nineteenth century, was born in December, 1812, in Kerkyra (Corfu). He received his general education at his native island and at Bologna, and studied law and philosophy at the University of Paris, where he received the degree of Doctor of Laws. When he returned to Kerkyra, in 1835, he assumed various public services and also occupied himself with patriotic journalism. In 1850 he was elected member of the Ionian Parliament. Later he was re-elected to the Parliament and proclaimed its president. From 1854 to 1864 he was professor of philosophy at the Ionian University in Kerkyra. In 1865 he was appointed State Adviser of Greece and Minister of Foreign Affairs. The same year he founded at Athens, together with other prominent men of letters, the society "Athenaion," whose declared purpose was the education of the people. From 1867 he served in succession as ambassador of Greece in London, Petrograd, Paris, and again in London, where he died on September 7, 1884. Throughout his political career he devoted his leisure to writing philosophical works.

His chief publications are the following:

(1) *Peri Prōtōn Ideōn kai Archōn Dokimion* ("Essay Concerning First Ideas and Principles"), Kerkyra, 1851, Athens, 1910.

(2) *Theōrētikēs kai Praktikēs Philosophias Stoicheia* ("Elements of Theoretical and Practical Philosophy"), Kerkyra, 1863, Athens, 1910.

(3) *Philosophikai Meletai* ("Philosophical Studies"), Kerkyra, 1864.

(4) *To Hen, to On, ē hē henotēs tēs Epistēmēs* ("The One, Being, or the Unity of Knowledge"), Kerkyra, 1870.

(5) *Peri tēs Henotētos tōn Logikōn Stoicheiōn* ("On the Unity of the Logical Elements"), Kerkyra, 1875, Athens, 1910.

(6) *Peri Psychēs, Theou, kai Ethikou Nomou Diatribai* ("Studies on the Soul, God, and Moral Law"), Constantinople, 1879.

(7) *Philotheou kai Eugeniou Epistolai, ētoi Syntomos Didaskalia peri Psychēs kai Theou* ("Letters of Philotheos and Eugene, or a Brief Teaching on the Soul and God"), Athens, 1884.

Vrailas' publications won him recognition not only in Greece, but also in other countries. Thus, he was elected a member of the Academy of the Moral and Political Sciences at Paris, honorary president of Copenhagen's Royal Society of Archeologists of the North, and a member of the Society for the Dissemination of Religious Knowledge at Petrograd, and of other similar institutions.

Like Benjamin, Vrailas-Armenis did not follow some one school of philosophy. He developed an eclectic system of philosophy, embracing an ontology, theology, psychology, philosophy of history, logic, aesthetics and ethics, using as his guides introspection and sense-observation, rational insight and deduction, and the light of his Orthodox Christian faith. His philosophy is distinguished by the persistent attempt to reconcile science with metaphysics, sense-experience and reason with religious faith. He and Skaltsounis are the most remarkable critics of materialism in Greece during the nineteenth century.

# Vrailas-Armenis

1. ON THE NATURE OF THE SOUL[1]

This question is very ancient. Aristotle viewed the soul as the principle of life and movement, and named it an *entelechy*. But before him Plato demonstrated the immateriality and immortality of the soul by means of all kinds of arguments, to which philosophy today can add little.

Medieval and modern philosophy also posed the question. But it must be admitted that this question, like that of existence and nature of God, was presented under a new aspect and was illuminated by a new light through the revelation of the Gospel.

In what follows, we shall consider whether the soul is a function of the body, or is a distinct and different substance, even though it is in a body; and what the nature of this substance is.

If the soul were a function of the body, it would have been a product of the organism. In that case we do not understand why this soul does not exist also in the organism of certain animals, which differ from the human organism only in insignificant respects. It is true that the latter is more perfect than the others, but the difference between it and the organisms immediately beneath it is by no means comparable to the difference between the in-

---

[1] From the book *Theoretikes kai Praktikes Philosophias Stoicheia*, Kerkyra, 1863, pp. 242-249.

telligence of man and the intelligence of the most perfect of the other animals. Regardless of the organism, there is an unbridgeable chasm between man and the irrational animals, even the most intelligent of them. If the soul were a function of the body, it should be studied, explained, and clarified like all the other functions of the body, through anatomical analysis and the laws of physiology. Yet, without inner observation, these contribute little or nothing to the knowledge of the soul. Finally, if it were a function of the body, it would have depended always and in all respects on it, like the other functions; but we observe the opposite. It is true that there are certain mutual relations of action between them, a parallelism in their development and decline; but the reverse course is also observed. At the very moment when the decline and deterioration of one of these sets in, the other begins to mature and amazingly to become more perfect.[2] The understanding is sometimes more perfect in direct proportion to the weakness of the organs. And certain factors, while causing the body to decay, vivify the spirit.[3]

Further, if we compare the attributes of matter in general with the attributes of the soul, we become even more convinced that the soul is of an opposite nature. Matter is extended and susceptible of motion. Extension is three-dimensionality. It fills a part of space through its particular dimensions, and seems infinitely divisible. The soul, on the other hand, has no extension, but is an indivisible unity. Thus there is no comparison between the phenomena of extension and those of mentality, which is the essential character of the soul. As far as motion is concerned, in the case of the body it is the passage from one point of space

---

[2] Plato remarks in his *Laws* that inner vision grows keener with age. "Every man when he is young," he says, "has that sort of vision dullest, and when he is old keenest" (IV, 715d-e). Similarly, Emerson observes: "The soul does not age with the body. On the borders of the grave, the wise man looks forward with equal elasticity of mind, or hope; . . for it is the nature of intelligent beings to be forever new to life" (*Letters and Social Aims*, p. 321).

[3] Thomas Mann makes a similar observation. Speaking of Dostoievsky, who had epileptic fits since his childhood, Mann remarks: "Certain attainments of the soul and the intellect are impossible without disease, . . . and the great invalids are crucified victims, sacrificed to humanity and its advancement, to the broadening of its feeling and knowledge" (*The Short Novels of Dostoevsky*, New York, 1945, p. xv).

## Nature of the Soul

to another; whereas the motion of the soul is not the passage from one point of space to another: the soul is an unmoved source of motion, an unmoved mover. Matter, being by nature inert, receives its motion through transmission. Spirit, on the other hand, is self-active, is originative of its motion. In matter, motion is transmitted in accordance with certain necessary laws, whereas the soul transmits it freely. . . .

Besides unity and self-activity, the soul has the attribute of consciousness of itself. The subject and the object of knowledge are here identical, and for this reason such knowledge has a clarity and certainty that are incontrovertible.[4] But such an identity is impossible in matter, where one point is juxtaposed to another; it is possible only in an immaterial substance. Therefore, consciousness, too, proves the immateriality of the soul.

Moreover, the soul knows all the other things by means of its own powers. The mind is the totality of the cognitive powers, namely, sense-perception, attention, abstraction, association, memory, and imagination. Each of these powers, while receiving in part the occasion for its activity from matter, does not originate at all from matter, and is not regulated by it. The material impression does not suffice for sense-perception: a certain inner awareness is needed. Attention is an endeavor of the soul towards strengthening sense-perception or consciousness. Abstraction is likewise an activity of the soul. Association is made in accordance with certain laws of inner unity, of inner combination. Memory is the abiding of data at a certain inner point, when the material elements are no longer present. Finally, imagination increases the vividness of sense-data or invents new combinations, which matter does not provide. Hence each of these powers presupposes and requires a certain inner factor, different from matter, from which factor the power springs and by which it is regulated. And the totality of these powers confirms this proof, because it effects an incessant elaboration of the data provided by matter — relations

---

[4] Cf. Bergson: "The existence of which we are most assured and which we know best is unquestionably our own, for of every other object we have notions which may be considered external and superficial, whereas, or ourselves, our perception is internal and profound" (*Creative Evolution*, London, 1913, p. 1).

of harmony, mutual support, and extreme unity among them, which are inexplicable in terms of matter. Moreover, the activity of the mind rises to its highest point in proportion as it is freed from the bonds of the body.

Now the same unity that prevails in the mind is also manifested in action, and unites both of these functions into one and the same activity.

The bodily man, on the other hand, is characterized by duality: he has two lobes in the brain, two branches of nerves, and two sense-organs of sight and hearing. . . .

Thus, both with respect to thought and action spirit is shown to be different from matter, the soul different from the body. We may therefore reasonably conclude that it does not die when the body dies, but survives it. This, however, does not prove that the soul is immortal, because even though it is immaterial and survives the body, it could undergo another death, peculiar to it, that is, through the annihilation of its existence by divine omnipotence.

But we have no instance of such annihilation in this world, where all things change without by any means being annihilated. So it seems to us an inconceivable and incomprehensible miracle, greater than creation itself. We merely take it as a hypothesis and must see if we can find a sufficient reason in Divine Providence to confirm it. In the part of this book dealing with Theology,[5] we saw that the Divine nature is all-powerful, all-wise, and all-good; and creates what is best; and we found that the purpose of the creation is the good of mankind. We have, therefore, no reason to assume the annihilation of the finest and most perfect creature of God, but on the contrary we see it destined for immortal life.

Now so far, following our definition of the soul, we compared each element of this creature, each attribute of the soul, with the attributes of matter, in order to show the opposition between them. But we omitted the foremost and chiefest attribute, which we placed at the beginning of the definition earlier in this book: rationality. Reason is the principle and law of the psychical powers. . . . Through reason we discover the real order of things, and grasp the notions of truth, beauty, and goodness — these three

---

[5] Pp. 175-212.

objects of man's intellectual and ethical activities. The soul tends incessantly toward these; and in this tendency the body is more an obstacle than an instrument, as disciplined abstraction, artistic inspiration and the yearning for the good prove. Considered essentially and in themselves, these three objects of man's intellectual and ethical activities are infinite attributes of the Infinite Being; and thus the soul tends with all its faculties towards infinite Truth, infinite Beauty, and infinite Goodness.[6] Now if the soul tends towards the Infinite, it necessarily has been destined to an immortal life, having been created in the image and likeness of the Infinite. Otherwise the rational and the ethical orders are not fulfilled, and there is a contradiction, an absurdity, an injustice as regards the finest and most perfect work of the all-powerful, all-wise and all-good God. . . .

The immortality of the soul is also proved by history. History would be a purposeless, incomprehensible, and inexplicable series of struggles and endeavors, if the individuals in it had no destiny and purpose higher than the earthly life. . . .

Thus, everything proves that the present life is only a preparation and testing for the enjoyment of the future life, a meditation on death, as Plato said, a process of self-perfecting, a keeping of the moral order at present with a view to attaining its consummation in the future.

## 2. SCIENCE AND THE SOUL[7]

There is today a kind of science that presents pernicious conclusions, that leads to absolute skepticism and inconsolable despair. There is a kind of science which holds that there is neither God nor soul, and the very ideas of an infinite and perfect Being and of a spiritual substance in us are absurd, self-contradictory, and incomprehensible. But this science is superficial, arbitrary, and imperfect. None of the natural sciences rightly understood and

---

[6] In *Philotheou kai Eugeniou Epistolai* (Athens, 1884), Vrailas-Armenis remarks: "True philosophy is a meditation on God, and true life is the ascent towards Him" (p. 281). As we perfect ourselves, "we become what we ought to be, children of God, destined to union with Him and blessedness" (p. 284).

[7] From *Philotheou kai Eugeniou Epistolai,* pp. 7-9, 17-18, 168-170.

confined within its own legitimate domain claims to destroy these eternal beliefs of mankind. This is proved by the fact that the greatest mathematicians, physicists, physiologists, and astronomers of the age that preceded ours, the very fathers of the physico-mathematical sciences, and the most famous representatives of these sciences in our time do not reject these beliefs, but on the contrary publicly profess and confess them.

As far as the ancients are concerned, I refer you to Socrates, Plato, and Aristotle, whose doctrines are far removed from the hopeless theories of our contemporary scepticism, and lead to the opposite convictions. As regards those immediately prior to the present age, it would be well to read a small work by Ernest Naville entitled *La Philosophie des fondateurs de la physique* (in the Bibliotheque Universelle of Geneva).[8] And as regards those of the present day, it is enough to mention the great names of Cauchy, Ampere, Dumas, and Pasteur, to whom not a few others should be added that hold a second place among those who cultivate the sciences of nature, who similarly do not deny either God or the soul, and detest materialism and the despair which it engenders. . . .

The error of pseudo science comes from two sources: from the misconception and unreasonable extension of the recent results of the sciences that pertain to matter, and from a certain philosophy known as positivism. The latter disregards the object, method, and purpose of true philosophy, and seeks to identify itself with the natural sciences, in order thus to invest its own theories with the precision, the clarity, and the certainty of the physico-mathematical sciences; and in this way it distorts them and destroys itself. . . ."[9]

---

[8] This study is contained in Naville's Book *La Physique Moderne,* Paris, 1883. Naville calls attention to the religious beliefs of scientists of the first order — the founders of modern physics — and the influence which these beliefs had on the directive principles of physics. These scientists were Copernicus, Kepler, Bacon, Descartes, Galileo, Newton, Leibniz, Laplace, Ampere, Liebig, Fresnel, Faraday, Mayer.

[9] This statement reminds one of the concluding remark which Whitehead makes in his Ingersoll Lecture on Immortality: "The final outlook of Philosophic thought," says Whitehead, "cannot be based upon the exact statements which form the basis of special sciences. The exactness is a fake" (Paul A. Schilpp, ed., *The Philosophy of Alfred North Whitehead,* Evanston and Chicago, 1941, p. 700).

## Science and the Soul

The science of matter explains in an excellent manner the laws of material nature, the material conditions and the material instruments of the intellect. But it explains none of the phenomena of the intellect. Nor does it explain what immediately accompanies the sense-impressions, that is, sensation, because it does not know what sensation is, how the impression is transformed into sensation, and how perception is engendered. . . . Moreover, physiology provides us with nothing certain regarding the principle of life in plants and animals.[10] Therefore, it is not justified in demanding from psychology the solution of the problem of the relationship between the soul and the body, so long as the problem regarding the principle of life remains unsolved. These things being so, what philosophy can that be which confines itself solely to the phenomena apprehended by the senses and to the necessary succession of such phenomena, which views man as a material organism and nothing else, which excludes *a priori* everything immaterial and spiritual, every search for first causes and ultimate purposes, in other words, reason itself, and which views the Infinity in which we live, by which we were brought into existence, and towards which we tend, as altogether unknowable and incomprehensible?

Positivism may be encyclopedic knowledge and a more or less successful systematization of the natural sciences; but it is never true philosophy. Philosophy does not follow the natural sciences but leads them,[11] because it studies the mind, through which and

---

[10] What Vrailas-Armenis said more than eighty years ago can be repeated today. The eminent American biologist Edmund W. Sinnott, for instance, remarks in one of his recent publications: "The quality of directive self-regulation, whatever its final relation to chemical and physical processes may prove to be, is a uniquely biological phenomenon, and an understanding of it, I believe, will provide a clue to the character of life itself. To explain it presents a problem of extraordinary difficulty and one must admit that little progress here has yet been made, a fact that often embarrasses botanists and zoologists, for it continues to lurk like a skeleton in the biological closet" (*Matter, Mind and Man,* New York, 1957, p. 39).

[11] Whitehead points this out with regard to induction, which is used by the natural sciences. "Induction," he observes, "presupposes metaphysics. In other words, it rests upon an antecedent rationalism. You cannot have a

from which comes every science, and to which it provides the object and the method.

---

rational justification for your appeal to history till your metaphysics has assured you that there *is* a history to appeal to; and likewise your conjectures as to the future presuppose some basis of knowledge that there *is* a future already subjected to some determination" (*Science and the Modern World*, p. 46).

# III

## IOANNIS SKALTSOUNIS

(1824-1905)

Ioannis Skaltsounis

# BIOGRAPHICAL NOTE ON SKALTSOUNIS

Ioannis Skaltsounis, one of the most eminent jurists and philosophers of modern Greece, was born in Lexouri, Kephallenia (Cephalonia) in 1824. He received his general education here. Then he studied law at the Ionian University and at the University of Pisa, where he took the degree of Doctor of Laws. After completing his studies, he stayed in Italy, at the cities of Florence, Venice, and Trieste, for a number of years. Subsequently he worked as director of insurance companies at Kephallonia, Athens, and Constantinople. In 1880 he was appointed president of the committee that was entrusted with the task of drawing up a civil and penal code for liberated Crete, the largest island of Greece. Skaltsounis worked very diligently for many years in preparing this code. He was also appointed a judicial advisor of the island in the city of Canea. His professional activities far from absorbed all his energies: throughout his long professional career he devoted his leisure to an assiduous study of the natural sciences, philosophy, and religion, especially his own — the Greek Orthodox — with a view to enlightening both himself and his fellow men. Thus, although he wrote works in the fields of economics and law, he also authored works in philosophy, particularly with regard to the relationships between science and religion. And it is for the latter writings that he is best known. He died in Crete on February 5, 1905.

The chief philosophical works of Skaltsounis are the following:

(1) *L'Huomo e il Materialismo,* Trieste, 1877, Milan, 1882.

(2) *Thrēskeia kai Epistēmē* ("Religion and Science"), Trieste, 1884.

(3) *Psychologikai Meletai* ("Psychological Studies"), Athens, 1889.

(4) *Peri Geneseōs tou Anthrōpou* ("Concerning the Genesis of Man"), Athens, 1893.

(5) *Thrēskeia kai Epistēmē: Dēmōdēs tou Christianismou Apologētikē* ("Religion and Science: Popular Apologetics of Christianity"), Athens, 1898.

These books, which are addressed to every intelligent reader and not to specialists alone, made Skaltsounis a very popular figure in Greece, and resulted in his receiving many honors. Enthusiastic reports about them spread beyond the boundaries of Greece, and *Religion and Science* was translated into Russian and published in the theological journal of the Academy of Petrograd, while *Concerning the Genesis of Man* was translated into Bulgarian and Italian.

In the above listed publications, which evince a remarkable familiarity with modern science, ancient and modern philosophy, and Christianity, Skaltsounis subjects materialism to unrelenting and penetrating criticism, and seeks to show that there is a harmony between true science, philosophy, and religion. He refutes, on philosophical and scientific grounds, the contention that the advances made by modern science have disproved religious doctrines, such as those of the existence of God, creation, and the immortality of the soul.

# *Skaltsounis*

## 1. CRITICISM OF MATERIALISM[1]

Our literature has already acquired a whole series of writings that deal widely with cosmological and anthropological subjects according to the principles and spirit of materialism and of every sort of scepticism and pessimism. Büchner's work *Force and Matter* was translated and published; and from it our youth learned that the universe has been produced spontaneously through the fortuitous collision and union of atoms moving in space from eternity. This publication has been followed by others, which teach the apelike ancestry of man and the spontaneous generation of life from inorganic matter. Through his recently published "Medical, Sociological and Philosophical Studies," under the title, *Psychoses*, Mr. Apostolidis[2] informs the Greek public of the research and inquiries conducted at insane asylums, as well as of the conclusions at which Jules Soury arrived through his psychiatric and philosophical investigations. According to these, man is a bodily machine devoid of every psychical and spiritual power and principle, moved by stimuli from external objects or by the automatic movements of the cells and organs composing it, and functioning according to the laws of general mechanics, like every other organic body. The powers of reasoning, knowing, willing, and so on, mental events, and even ultramundane insights, the aspiration towards

---
   1  From *Psychologikai Meletai,* Athens, 1889, pp. 5-7, 451-455, 458-461.
   2  Simon Apostolidis, a physician. His book appeared in 1889. Skaltsounis thought it was the most pernicious book that had appeared in Greece and hence undertook at once to refute its materialistic theses. The result was his *Psychologikai Meletai.*

ideals, the feelings of our inmost consciousness, as well as every noble and lofty belief and every virtue and act of self-denial depend exclusively upon the vibrations of the nerves of the cerebral region. And, according to the teaching of the author of *Psychoses,* our convictions about a spiritual principle and power in us lack all objective reality and substance . . .

According to Büchner and according to the views and opinions of Jules Soury, which our author of *Psychoses* shares, there exists only one science,[3] there exists only one series of events, one ground of things, that which springs from the vibrations of bodies; while psychical and spiritual phenomena are a reflection of the spontaneous change and movement of the cells of the cerebral matter; and the belief in the spirituality of the soul must be discarded, inasmuch as no one can understand the existence of a power independent of, and separate from, matter.

"The foundation of the knowledge of things lies," according to the author of *Psychoses,* "in the anatomical and physiological conditions of the brain" (p. 114).

However, by a strange contradiction the same author assures us that "the mechanism of the brain is unknown in its particulars" (p. 259); and "how it happens that the vibration of the particles of matter is manifested as sensation and the perception of things, that is, receives a subjective or psychical character," is something incomprehensible to the human mind (p. 109). And according to the assertions of the most eminent anatomists, physiologists, and psychiatrists, particularly of Krafft-Ebing, the architecture of the brain and its physiological functions remain hidden in dense and very deep darkness.

And yet, in the midst of such an uncertainty and ignorance within the anatomical sciences, the materialists dare to disturb the religious and moral principles of peoples, to ask them to discard the universal convictions that are sanctioned by ancient and modern knowledge and by the logic of things, and replace them by a monstrous theory according to which mental events spring from the mechanical vibrations of the cerebral cells. Discard, they tell

---

[3] *Viz.,* mechanics.

us, the belief in the existence of an incorporeal power within us, because it is impossible to conceive of the existence of a power not dependent upon and emanating from matter; accept, instead, our proposition which asserts the emanation of mental phenomena from the vibrations of bodily particles, which emanation we are the first to admit and state is incomprehensible to the human intellect! Believe in our declarations about the properties and activities of the mechanism of the brain, which we picture with geometrical figures, but do not ask us for any information or clarification regarding this mechanism, because it is unknown to us in its details, while to other scientists it is unknown both in its details and as a whole! Abandon all the declarations of the philosophical and other mental sciences, and accept only the doctrines and theories of the positive sciences. And, rejecting the declarations of Aristotle, Bacon, Humbolt, Haller, Faraday, Chevreul, Davy, and all the most eminent teachers of the physical sciences, follow the whims of Büchner and Jules Soury!

But before applying yourselves to the work of spreading your theories to the multitudes and to the youth of your country, should you not have waited until the scientific discussion of the questions that have arisen had been exhausted, or at least until some of the distinguished scientists had accepted them as sound? On the very day when you were telling the Greek public that the question about the soul has been definitively settled in accordance with the materialistic view, in France the great Ampere, who applied the theories of electricity to telegraphy and to all sorts of other things useful in everyday life, taught that after having submitted the psychological problem to analysis and study, as he had submitted the problems about physical reality, and having studied for a long time all the hypotheses that had been proposed, he came to the conclusion that only one hypothesis is in agreement and harmony with the facts, the doctrine of Christian philosophy. The next day, Huxley, the prop of the materialists in England, deserting those who were of the same mind as he, cried out: "You, Büchner, repeat with great bombast and pomp that 'matter and force' are all that exists, and that there exists no power independent of matter. But what are we to say to those who have a contrary opinion, when they present us the power and activities of self-consciousness?"[4]

In addition, pathologists, physiologists, anatomists, physicians, and vivisectors have taught us principles and made declarations quite contrary to those of the materialists. And those who do not mix pathological and anatomical with psychological and moral questions have assured us that the positive sciences, being unqualified to solve questions pertaining to the first principle and essence of things, know nothing about the hypothetical vibrations of the cells, from which, according to the teachings of the materialists, psychological phenomena are produced independently of every spiritual power.

Thus, supported by the words of distinguished physiologists and pathologists, and by the declarations or science, we can confidently say to the physicians and naturalists in Greece who are struggling to persuade us that we are but unconscious machines, governed by the fateful law of bodies:

"Gentlemen! You know nothing about what you are teaching us, because the science in whose name you are speaking knows nothing about these things. Physicians and naturalists, you are altogether unqualified, in your capacity as physicians and naturalists, to solve spiritual and supraorganic questions; for the leaders of the physical and nosological sciences have declared themselves unqualified to solve them. And we push aside and reject and annihilate by means of invincible scientific authority all the declar-

---

[4] Among those who stressed the existence of consciousness as a standing refutation of materialism was Huxley's friend John Fiske. In one of his books, which was published five years before Skaltsounis' *Psychologikai Meletai*, from which this text has been taken, Fiske says: That consciousness "cannot possibly be the product of any cunning arrangement of material particles is demonstrated beyond peradventure by what we know of the correlation of material forces. The Platonic view of the soul, as a spiritual substance, an affluence from Godhood, which under certain conditions becomes incarnated in perishable forms of matter, is doubtless the view most consonant with the present state of our knowledge" (*The Destiny of Man,* Boston and New York, 1884, pp. 42-43). Similarly, fifteen years later he remarked: "Of all realities the soul is the most solid, sound, and undeniable. Thoughts and feelings are the fundamental facts from which there is no escaping. . . . Consciousness, the soul's fundamental fact, is the most fundamental of facts. But a truly marvellous affair is consciousness!" (*Through Nature to God,* Boston and New York, 1899, pp. 27-28).

ations about the soul made by the materialists among you. Do not forget that in 1889 the most eminent anatomist of Europe and the most distinguished psychiatrist of Germany[5] admitted that the statement made by the learned Italian physician about the ignorance and darkness that exists in the positive sciences regarding the structure and functions of the cerebral matter is still indisputable: *"Obscura textura, obscuriores functiones, morbi obscurisimi."*[6]

Now in the face of this strange endeavor to subject the study of mental phenomena and questions to the sciences of the mechanics of bodies, in the midst of the acknowledged ignorance and incompetence of the physical and physiological sciences as regards the subjects in question, and in the midst of the disputes of the students of the brain and nosologists, a resplendent light illuminates the question about the essence of the soul. A manifest fact attested by all solves the dispute that is raised by the materialist and puts and end to every further discussion. Man's freedom of directing his powers of cognition and volition, his moral freedom and the responsibility which arises from it — the freedom of the human personality — this is the weighty fact, the fundamental distinguishing mark of human existence, the resplendent light that dispels the mist and the darkness of the horrible teachings of materialism.

And let us repeat here a truth that springs from this incontrovertible fact and indeed is identifiable with it. Freedom of the cognitive activity, freedom of directing the attention of the cognitive faculties, freedom of the will and moral responsibility — these are a negation of mechanism, a negation of the corporeality

---

[5] Namely, Krafft-Ebing.

[6] "Its structure is obscure, its functions are more obscure, and its diseases are most obscure." This statement still holds today, so far as the relation of the brain to mental events is concerned. Thus, Professor Roger W. Sperry, who is an authority on the functional architecture of the brain, has recently remarked: "The centermost processes of the brain with which consciousness is presumably associated are simply not understood. They are so far beyond our comprehension at present that no one I know of has been able even to imagine their nature. . . . The great in-between realm, starting at the stage where the incoming excitatory messages first reach the cortical surfaces of the brain, still today is very aptly referred to as the 'mysterious black box' " (Mind, Brain, and Humanist Values," in *New Views of the Nature of Man*, ed. by John R. Platt, Chicago and London, 1965, pp. 76-77).

of the soul, an invincible proof of the existence of an unseen world and of spiritual powers that are independent of the unconscious, ineluctable and unchangeable laws of the palpable and visible world.[7]

## 2. SPIRITUAL NATURE OF THE SOUL[8]

Analyzing the elements that together constitute my personality and substance, I am conscious that there exists in me a power in which there are gathered my emotional states and changes, from which, as a single and indivisible center, there proceed my intellectual and moral activities, and at which there meet all insights and functions of my spiritual life. My body is circumscribed within a very limited space, and my bodily powers act on things so far as the mechanical movement of my hands and of the tools I use extends. . . . But the mysterious center of my spiritual substance has different characteristics, contrary to the mechanical.

Confined in my study, I traverse mentally land and sea and countries I have never visited, and think about and judge peoples I have never seen. Meditating on wholly ideal or theoretical subjects, not encountered in the tangible and visible world, I form within myself ideas having no corporeal character and not representing anything material or bodily. I turn my thoughts to the beautiful and create in my imagination images remote from reality, or invent an interweaving of passions and ideas which I express through speech or writing. I admire the virtues of self-denial of those who have overcome all bodily instincts and offered their very existence for the sake of a noble aspiration and conviction. I

---

[7] In his defense of the soul's essential independence of the body and its immortality, William Ernest Hocking similarly stresses the significance of freedom. "If the human mind or soul is capable of what we call a free choice," says Hocking, "it is, in that small chink of the universe, standing for a moment outside the stream of cause and effect and determining what Nature shall contain. In principle, the body is there dependent on the mind, not the mind on the body. And if this is the case in that small chink of the universe, we have there an insight into the way things are put together. We can see that in its own character the physical world, which destroys the body, cannot destroy what is free from the body" ("Immortality in the Light of Science and Philosophy," in *Man's Destiny in Eternity: The Garvin Lectures*, Boston, 1949, p. 159).

[8] From *Peri Geneseos tou Anthropou*, Athens, 1893, pp. 257-260, 265-266.

make judgments about the impressions that are transmitted to my brain through the sense-organs of my body, and experience the pleasure or pain that comes from them. I cognize, will, doubt, am persuaded, and decide. And I feel that all these activities are performed by the inner power in me which is conscious both of these activities and of its unity and identity. And what is most important of all, this same power often clashes and wrestles with the inclinations and appetites of the body; and persisting in its decisions, it overcomes every inclination, every instinct, every mechanical law; and as an absolute master and ruler, it imposes upon the body movements and actions which the body performs in the face of all kinds of pain and hardship.

Every human being is conscious of this mysterious and at the same time manifest power; and mankind, before every religious dogma and every scientific theory, guided by its own consciousness and as by an innate insight, characterized it as having neither a material substratum, nor mass, nor weight, nor extension. And having made their inquiries with this insight as their foundation, all the great minds of ancient and modern times, and all eminent students of man and discoverers of the laws of nature have confirmed this universal belief and called the unitary and spiritual power in us the *soul* (*psyche*), and have regarded it as constituting the basis and essence of human personality, rising as far as the infinite and filled with ultramundane feelings and convictions.

Neither the consciousness of mankind, nor the profundity of the knowledge of the wise have defined the modes of the activities of the spirit within us and the mysterious bonds through which it is united and consorts with the body. But the ignorance concerning the ways in which it acts has not at all shaken the steadfast belief about the spiritual and immaterial attributes of the soul. This belief, which illuminates mankind in the development of its potentialities and is the foundation stone of all perfection in knowledge and moral character, resembles the belief in the existence of the sun, which provides us with light and warmth and every kind of blessing, and about whose existence we have no doubt at all, even though we are ignorant both about the ways in which it acts and about its inmost essence and substance. And just as there have been sophists who have disputed the objective existence of the sun, and have attributed the ideas and beliefs about the visible world to illusion, so there have appeared from time to time men who have disputed the existence of a spiritual power in us. And in our days, the doctrines of materialism, having donned the robe of science, are taught by amateurs of science as the final conclusions of scientific research.

Let no one say that, although we are ignorant about the essence of the sun, we nevertheless know about its existence through the impressions made upon our organs of vision by its visible rays; for the testimony of our consciousness in confirming the existence of the power which acts in us is an insight that is surer than every external activity, while the spiritual character of the center which constitutes our personality is not only known by consciousness and insight, but is also demonstrated by all its manifestations and functions.

The philosophy of ancient Greece, as well as that of the last centuries and of our time, draws its proofs of the spirituality of the center of human personality from the unity of consciousness and of all the activities of the understanding and the will. We would produce a whole library if we were to undertake to give even a brief account of the ideas and convictions of every philosophical genius on this subject, from Aristotle to Leibniz and Cousin, in order to confirm our principles and declarations. . . .

But what need is there of invoking the views and authority of famous philosophers and scientists? Does not the consciousness of each one of us testify that there exist in us powers united with the body in an incomprehensible manner, and working in a way altogether different from, and opposed to, the mechanicalness of the laws of visible and tangible nature? We are present at a large gathering, where an orchestra delights the hearing of the audience; and yet in the midst of the sounds that affect our hearing as well as that of the others, we do not apprehend the harmony at all, but turn our thoughts to the journey that we are planning, or muse upon some joyful or sad feeling. This phenomenon clearly shows the soundness of the philosophical principles regarding the spiritual nature of the substance in us that feels and thinks. The air waves produced by the musical instruments reach the ear and stimulate the auditory nerve; but in order that the impressions might enter into our inner sense and produce sound, the stimulation of the nerves of the sense-organs is not enough: the attention of the psyche is required, directed to the impression made upon the sense-organ and the nerves of the brain.

And observe the independence of our spirit from the circumstances surrounding us and from bodily impressions whenever we turn it away at will from every mechanical action. We live in the past and think about the future, which does not yet exist.[9] We live in world of ideas, which a Creator has made or which we have made through our imagination. We separate ourselves from the objects about us and from our very bodily and organic existence, and make our personality at once the subject and the object of study. With our intellect we analyze our cognitive and moral powers and capacities, and work independently of every sense-impression.

Observe also that our spirit is not always where our body is, but is where it thinks, where it acts, where it loves, often simultaneously at many points and in relation to many subjects. It is with God whenever it worships God. It is with our fellows near and far away. It lives with the living and associates with those who have departed, and in general it functions in ways remote from the laws of mechanicalness.

### 3. IMMORTALITY OF THE SOUL[10]

Whoever has formed firm convictions concerning the creation of man and his spiritual and free hypostasis, sees the future life as all the great minds of mankind have seen it, from Socrates to Victor Hugo,[11] independently of all religious doctrines. "Those who do not believe in the immateriality and imperishability of the

---

[9] Cf. Bergson: "When we speak of mind we mean, above everything else, consciousness. . . . All consciousness is memory, — conservation and accumulation of the past in the present. But all consciousness is also anticipation of the future. Consider the direction of your mind at any moment you like to choose; you will find that it is occupied with what now is, but always and especially with regard to what is about to be" (*Mind-Energy*, trans. by M. Wildon Carr, New York, 1920, pp. 7-8.)

[10] From *Peri Geneseos tou Anthropou*, pp. 530-531.

soul have not been present at the death of a genius; but I have been," wrote the distinguished Arsene Houssaie. "How many times didn't I hear Hugo proclaiming and teaching the immortality of the soul! One evening he seemed to be asleep; but suddenly he raised his head and opened his still sparkling eyes. 'I am not asleep,' he said, 'but hear what is being said around me and most of all what is being said above us. Everything is luminous in my head; the earth still provides me with its saps, but a heavenly light of other worlds shines in my spirit. Perhaps you believe that the soul is a product of organic and bodily movements and functions. But then why is the mind brighter at this moment, when the powers of the body are vanishing? A heavy winter has come upon my bodily organism, but an eternal spring is preserved in my soul. The more I approach the end, the more clearly I discern the heavenly harmonies. For half a century I have been writing my ideas. I applied myself to history, philosophy, legends, traditions, songs, to everything knowable. Yet I have not expended even a thousandth part of the spiritual life within me. In the grave I will not say that I have ceased living, but that I have ended my day — for the new one begins the next day. The grave is not the end, but simply a transition."[12]

Not all, however, are gifted with the power of Socratic or Platonic dialectic in order to ascertain through logic the truth about the immortality of the soul. . . . Not all are able through transcendent thoughts and metaphysical theorems to infer the truth about the future life from the moral law. And quite rare are the minds that are gifted with genius and intuit eternity and hear the heavenly harmonies, such as Franklin, Leibniz, and Maine de Biran. But all those who believe in Christ accept as absolute truth the dogmas about the creation, destiny, and immortality of man, independently of all scientific or metaphysical elaboration. And the doctrines of the Faith, by unfolding man's innate religious consciousness, enlighten and at the same time strengthen it, and transform it into an unconquerable power.

---

[11] Cf. K. Jaspers: "A mere historic fact will give us pause: for thousands of years, the best and wisest of men have believed in immortality" (*Philosophy and the World*, trans. by E. B. Ashton, Chicago, 1963, p. 135).

[12] *Evénement*, June 2, 1885. Arsène Houssaie. (Skaltsounis' note.)

# IV

# ST. NECTARIOS KEPHALAS

(1846 - 1920)

St. Nectarios Kephalas

# BIOGRAPHICAL NOTE ON ST. NECTARIOS

This very eminent theologian-philosopher was born on October 1, 1846, at Silyvria, Eastern Thrace. At the age of fourteen he went to Constantinople, where he was engaged as a store clerk by one of his relatives. Having an ardent desire for learning, he did not stay at this job for long. He found employment as an overseer of children at a Greek school, where he had the opportunity of attending the higher grades and teaching the lower ones. At the age of twenty he left Constantinople and went to the island of Chios. Here he was appointed a teacher at the elementary school in the village of Lythi. After teaching at Lythi for seven years, he entered Chios' famous Byzantine Monastery of Nea Moni. He stayed at Nea Moni for three years, which he devoted largely to self-education. Wishing to further his education in a more systematic manner, he went to Athens and entered the School of Theology of Athens University. When he received the degree of Licentiate in Theology, he left for Alexandria, at the invitation of the Patriarch of that city. The Patriarch ordained Nectarios a Presbyter in 1886 and Metropolitan of Pentapolis in 1889. Local intrigues resulted in his being removed from the Orthodox Church of Egypt in 1890, on groundless charges. He returned to Greece, where the Ministry of Church Affairs appointed him in 1891 preacher and in 1894 head of the Rizarios Ecclesiastical School at Athens. He remained director of the school until 1908, when he resigned in order to spend rest of his life in prayer, meditation, and writing at a convent in the island of Aegina, not far from Piraeus. Nectarios died on November 8, 1920. Regarded by many as a saint during his lifetime, he was canonized in 1961 by the Synod of the Ecumenical Patriarchate.

His publications include, besides many theological books, the following philosophico-religious ones:

(1) *Hypotypōsis peri Anthrōpou* ("Sketch Concerning Man"), Athens, 1893.

(2) *Peri Alēthous kai Pseudous Morphōseōs* ("Concerning True and Pseudo Education"), Athens, 1894.

(3) *Hierōn kai Philosophikōn Logiōn Thēsaurisma* ("A Treasury of Sacred and Philosophical Sayings"), Vol. I, Athens, 1895, Vol. II, Athens, 1896.

(4) *Meletē peri tēs Athanasias tēs Psychēs* ("Study Concerning the Immortality of the Soul"), Athens, 1901.

(5) *To Gnōthi Sauton* ("Self-Knowledge"), Athens, 1904, 1962.

Being simultaneously a philosopher and a theologian, St. Nectarios saw a harmony between true philosophy and revealed theology. The philosophy with which he was best acquainted was that of the ancient Greeks. And he explicitly adopted the view of Clement of Alexandria regarding it: that the ancient Greek philosophers grasped many truths concerning God, the soul and virtue, and that their teaching has helped the Greek race understand revealed truth, which is a guide of the highest value in the philosophic quest. Of all the philosophers, it is to Plato that Nectarios turns most, particularly in dealing with the question of the immortality of the soul. But he goes far beyond Plato in his proofs of immortality, which are of the nature of meditations.

# St. Nectarios

## 1. PROLEGOMENA CONCERNING THE IMMORTALITY OF THE SOUL[1]

"I am the God of Abraham, and the God of Isaac, and the God of Jacob. God is not the God of the dead, but of the living" (Matt. 22: 32). This truth, which is revealed to us by Holy Scripture, is the first doctrine that man ought to believe, in order to know himself: who he is, what the aim and purpose of his presence in this world is, and whither he is destined to go. Without the truth that has been revealed to him, man is incapable of knowing himself; for the lack of knowledge of revealed truth leads man to false theories or erroneous doctrines, and these lead to absurd inferences; for the mind alone is unable to uncover the mysteries. Revelation is the lamp that illuminates and guides the mind in its inquiries and leads it to the truth. While holding this lamp, we shall prove dialectically that man has an immortal soul. . . .

Revelation must be the basis in philosophizing, in order that philosophy might arrive at true conclusions. The philosopher must believe that he has received a living soul from God, in order that he might know it. Indeed, he already knows that there is in him something different from matter; but he does not know *what* it is. In order that cognition might become knowledge, faith in revealed truth is required. He who philosophizes must first believe in the spiritual nature that distinguishes him into knower and object known, and then seek to know it completely. The existence of the living soul is a solved problem for believers, but a hidden mystery

---

[1] From the book *Melete Peri tes Athanasias tes Psyches,* Athens, 1901, pp. 7-9, 11.

for unbelievers. Faith is the eye of the soul, which perceives itself and searches the unseen and the hidden. God revealed to man his noble origin and made known to him the immortality of his soul, in order to attract him towards Himself, to impel him towards virtue, and to lead him towards self-perfection. To discard revealed truth is to discard the purposeful and pre-ordained end of the world; for the purpose of the world is testified by the omniscience of the Creator, which created nothing purposeless. Man's perfection, which without a living soul is a pointless and impossible pursuit, is demanded by the purpose and pre-ordained end of the world; because without it the creation of man becomes a purposeless play.

Let no one say, great is man's egoism. For great indeed is the spiritual man,[2] too, who has been created in the image of his Creator God. Hence he is Godlike and God-inspired and receptive of divine revelation, and hence superior to the whole of created nature by virtue of his lofty origin, the nobility of his nature, and the character of his soul. His spirit rises towards God, is illumined by the divine light, puts off the mist of the darkness of matter and understands "what eye has not seen nor ear heard, nor entered into the heart of man."[3]

God dwells and moves in him. . . . He Who cannot be contained by the universe dwells mystically in the heart of microscopic man. It sounds strange, yet it is true. The manner is mystical, but His revelation is manifest from its results. God is infinite and the universe is in the palm of His hand, and man is a speck of dust; and yet he rises above the cosmos, above the heavens, and views with his mental eyes the grandeur of the creation, examines and searches the universe with his rational power, discovers the laws that govern the universe, measures the vast distances and dimensions of heavenly bodies, knows the density, solidity and quantity of the substances that make up the bodies, and in general the nature and the attractive and repulsive force of the enormous giants of the heavenly firmament.

---

[2] The inner man, the spirit or soul.
[3] 1 Cor. 2: 9.

Illuminated by the divine light, his intellect reaches the Creator of the universe, studies the character of the divine Creator, and makes assertions about His attributes. . . . Enlightened by the divine light and strengthened by divine grace, he becomes superior to all the irrational natures, and although clothed with earthly flesh, he rivals the nature of heavenly angels. . . .

Divine wisdom created man the head of creation, in order that he might apprehend and understand his divine Creator. . . . Man is the reason of the creation. Yes, man, God created you a god on earth. Sin and the withdrawal from God have deprived you of this knowledge. They have darkened your mind, which sees God. They have led you astray and cast you into the mire of the passions which have marred the brightness of the image. Yes, know that you are an image and likeness of God, and that you have an immortal soul, which is destined through grace to live eternally. Search yourself, in order to see and be convinced how many of your activities and works testify to the immortality of your soul.

## 2. PROOFS OF THE IMMORTALITY OF THE SOUL[4]

### (i) *Proof of the Immortality of the Soul from its Activities*

The rational soul of man occupies itself with intellectual theories, seeks the reason for its existence, rises to the idea of God and the necessity of His existence. These theories, being mental, must have a mental cause. This mental cause must be entirely different from matter. Now since the world in which man dwells is material, it is necessary that we refer the origin of the rational soul to another, immaterial world. This necessity obliges us to admit the immortality of such a soul, for death prevails only in the case of the bodies of the material world, whereas the soul, not being constituted of the matter of this world, is not subject to death.

---

[4] From *Melete Peri tes Athanasias tes Psyches*, pp. 36-66. Nectarios gives nineteen proofs. I have omitted the last proof (pp. 68-77), because of its length and the impossibility of abridging it. This proof is entitled: "Proof of the Immortality of the Soul from the Destiny of Nations and from Divine Providence, as Inferred from the Philosophy of History."

The mind rises to the notion of immaterial entities. If it were material in nature, it would have been incapable of grasping the ideas of immaterial things. The rational soul of man possesses the power not only of seeking things that are by nature ideal, but also of idealizing things entirely material, by stripping them of their material cover and viewing them as abstract ideas, and of rising through intuitive reason to universal ideas.

The soul is conscious of itself and conscious of its cognitions. The soul inquires into, and seeks to know, not only external objects, but also itself and its activities, and to judge itself and make assertions about the quality of its acts and activities. The soul not only treasures up within itself an immense number of truths, but also becomes itself a treasury of a vast number of laid up truths and perceives the absolute value of these truths and their action upon it. And further, it feels its natural kinship to supernatural truths and aspires to live in this spiritual world of truths. This testifies to its immortality.

Philosophers[5] say: Whatever is self-active and ever active is immortal. Hence the soul, being ever-active in and of itself, is immortal.

### (ii) *Proof of the Immortality of the Soul from its Aspirations*

The rational soul of man has supernatural aspirations, infinite aspirations. If the rational soul were dependent upon the body and died together with the body, it should necessarily submit to the body and follow it in all its appetites. Independence would have been contrary both to the laws of nature and to reason, because it disturbs the harmony between the body and the soul. As dependent upon the body it should submit to the body and follow it in all its appetites and desires, whereas, on the contrary, the soul masters the

---

[5] E.g. Plato (*Phaedrus,* 245c-e, *Laws,* X, 896a-b). Cf. St. Athanasius: "If as we have shown, the soul moves the body and is not moved by other things, it follows that the movement of the soul is spontaneous, and that this spontaneous movement goes on after the body is laid aside in the earth" (*A Select Library of Nicene and Post-Nicene Fathers,* Second Series, Vol. IV, New York, 1892, p. 21).

body, imposes its will upon the body. The soul subjugates and curbs the appetites and passions of the body, and directs them as it[6] wills. This phenomenon comes to the attention of every rational man; and whoever is conscious of his own rational soul is conscious of the soul's mastery over the body. The mastery of the soul over the body is proved by the obedience of the body when it is being led with self-denial to sacrifice for the sake of the abstract ideas of the soul. The domination by the soul and the condemnation of the body to death by the soul for the prevalence of its principles, ideas, and views would have been entirely incomprehensible if the soul died together with the body. But a mortal soul would never have risen to such a height, would never have condemned itself to death along with the body for the prevalence of abstract ideas that lacked meaning, since no noble idea, no noble courageous thought has any meaning for a mortal soul. A soul, therefore, which is capable of such things must be immortal.[7]

### (iii) *Historical Proof of the Immortality of the Soul*

The immortality of the soul is testified by the universal belief of nations in its immortality. Historical evidence shows that the whole human race has believed in the new life after death.[8] We find this hope as much among the barbaric and savage peoples as among the civilized. The fact that men of every epoch, of every place and every level of development accept a life after death and have hope in it is evidence of man's profound conviction in the immortality of his soul. This hope regarding immortality becomes an unshakable belief and develops to such an extent that all the moral activities come to spring from this belief. This phenomenon would have been impossible if the belief in the immortality of the soul were simply an expression of man's egoistic desire and was not grounded in the very nature of the human spirit and did not spring

---

[6] The soul.

[7] Cf. Jaspers: "The manifestations of love and the achievement of self-conquest bring man to an awareness in a reality that is more than transitory, empirically real — a reality which still resounds to the word immortality" (*Philosophy and the World*, p. 137).

[8] Many other philosophers have stressed this fact, among them Ralph Waldo Emerson and Karl Jaspers. Emerson remarks: "In the first records of

from the depths of man. Also, the sages of every epoch speak of the immortality of soul.

The Epicurean doctrines of the philosophers who in different periods have gone astray have always been repulsed by sound philosophy. The negation of the immortality of the soul would have attributed an extremely serious error to divine wisdom in inscribing such an illusion, such a chimera in the heart of man. If man were not immortal, he should not have had a rational soul, nor should he have been able to imagine immortality.

### (iv) *Metaphysical Proof of the Immortality of the Soul*

The immortality of the soul is testified by the study of the powers and distinctive attributes of the soul. The simplicity of the soul, the immateriality of its substance are indicative of its immortality. Also, its self-consciousness, its power of free choice and self-ruling (*autexousion*), and its freedom of cognition evince that the soul belongs to a spiritual world. Again, its aspiration to approach the infinitely perfect Being, its immanent purposefulness (*entelecheia*), and the perpetual activity of the spirit show that the soul is a living entity having no reason within itself to die, no reason to disintegrate or be dissolved; and hence they testify that the soul survives after its separation from the body and is immortal.

Plato proves the immortality of the soul above all from the simplicity and immateriality of its substance. And concerning its release from here he says the following:

"When death attacks a man, the mortal portion of him dies, but the immortal retires at the approach of death and is preserved

---

a nation in any degree thoughtful and cultivated, some belief in the life beyond would of course be suggested. . . . There never was a time when the doctrine of a future life was not held" (*Letters and Social Aims,* Boston, 1894, p. 308). And Jaspers says: "Most of us have always believed and still believe today that they will go on living [after death]. The faithful Christian trusts the pledges of the Bible. To the Hindu it is a matter of course that each soul has already lived in countless past forms of existence and will exist in new forms in the future; he believes in reincarnation. The primitives know that their dead appear as ghosts. The Greeks had a Feast of All Souls for entertaining the dead; it closed with an appeal to the souls to go back to the nether world. There would be no end to a compendium of the varied ways in which faith in a continuing life after death manifests itself throughout the world" (*Philosophy and the World,* p. 134).

sound and imperishable. Beyond question, then, the soul is immortal and imperishable. . . ."[9]

(v) *Teleological Proof of the Immortality of the Soul*

The rational soul of man, being a simple and immaterial substance and having such attributes for its development and perfection, for attaining a definite purposeful goal, must be immortal.

If man has a mortal soul, to what end does he have such attributes, to what end moral powers, to what end noble dispositions, to what end infinite aspirations and his whole spiritual and moral life? This problem is solved only by admitting the immortality of the soul. Without it, the events of man's spiritual and moral life are insoluble enigmas, and man's struggle in his ethical and spiritual life is a struggle without victory, and a striving without a purpose.

(vi) *Ethical Proof of the Immortality of the Soul*

The immortality of the soul is testified by its aspiration towards the supreme good. By supreme good we mean the final good, which is essentially and really superior to all other goods, and in which alone man finds moral calm, absolute peace of the soul and spiritual joy, through which his soul is filled with ineffable gladness. The final good contains the most perfect good, the fullness of goods, in which every longing is satisfied and every hope is fulfilled. This highest good is the Kingdom of God, which is spiritual communion, or the communion of God with men and a participation in the holiness, love, grace, and blessedness of God. This Kingdom of God man ardently desires and seeks, and struggles for it during his whole life on earth, and sacrifices all the goods of this world in order to enjoy it. But while man gives everything for the acquisition of the supreme good, he only enjoys a certain degree of moral happiness, because during his earthly life the reign of evil gives him innumerable occasions for sorrow. In this world it is impossible for man to become absolutely blessed, because the calm of his soul and the peace of his heart are often disturbed by dreadful bodily pains, the afflictions and sorrows of his neighbors, the rav-

---

[9] *Phaedo*, 106e.

ages and devastations brought on by wars, the harm caused by famine and plagues, the upheavals caused by earthquakes, the misfortunes of relatives and friends, and in general the sorrows that come from moral and material causes. These reduce the moral happiness of man in this life, while the longing for the supreme good remains unfulfilled. But this longing expresses a certain emptiness in the soul demanding fulfillment, as well as the idea of the possibility of its fulfillment. This necessity leads us to the conclusion that the soul, whose infinite aspirations remain unfulfilled in this world, will receive the fulfillment of the remaining emptiness within it after the end of this life and its entry into the eternal life, where the supreme good and absolute blessedness are found.

Also, the fulfillment of the yearning for the supreme good is imperfect in this world, and can only be realized here in a rather limited degree, not only where evil reigns, but also where virtue and holiness prevail, because even in the midst of the virtues the reign of evil reacts and fights against the Kingdom of God and sows tares in the wheat. Reason, therefore, demands that we admit that the perfect fulfillment of the aspiration towards the supreme good will take place in the future life, where absolute love, joy, and peace reign. The ardent desire for the supreme good thus testifies that it will be fulfilled in the future life and convinces us about the immortality of the soul of man.

We come to the same conclusion through a consideration of moral perfection, which the soul strives to attain by disciplining and subduing the body. The aspiration after moral perfection expresses a certain innate tendency of the rational soul towards elevating itself from this material world to another, spiritual world; it testifies to an unceasing progress directed to absolute perfection. But absolute perfection is found in the absolute life; and the absolute life, in the ultramundane world. Hence, moral perfection necessarily leads us to the absolute life, to immortality.

(vii) *The Immortality of the Soul Proved from the Goodness of the Divine Creator*

The whole of creation speaks of the goodness of God, Who

provides abundantly the means for happiness for those of His creatures that have consciousness. The happiness of man should have been complete, inasmuch as he has all the means and has at his disposal the whole created world. And yet his happiness is incomplete, for every day we see man grumbling and hear him speaking about his unhappiness. A boundless yearning possesses his heart, which, greatly afflicted by the remaining emptiness within it, incessantly seeks to fill it. Man struggles for the fulfillment of the demands of his heart, but his heart always remains empty. None of the goods on earth is sufficient to fill the emptiness of his heart; there is no counterpoise to his longing, his heart is afflicted; and happiness is remote. The reason for the insufficiency is found not in the nature of things, but in the soul that dwells in man, which, being immortal has infinite aspirations and hence ardently desires and seeks, like a thirsty deer, the enjoyment of the supreme good, which is its ultimate goal. . . . The all-good God would not have implanted in the heart of man an unfulfilled aspiration that renders him unhappy, unless He had reserved its fulfillment. Since it remains unfulfilled in this world, it follows that it will be fulfilled after man's departure from it, in the other life, where he will live happily and hence eternally. Thus the aspiration after the supreme good is a proof of the immortality of the soul.[10]

If man finds a certain relative happiness on earth, he finds it in the conviction that he has an immortal soul, and that after the end of the present life there is another life which is unceasing and endless, in which he will enjoy perfect happiness. If he finds a

---

[10] In the same vein, Emerson remarks: "There is nothing in nature capricious, or whimsical, or accidental, or unsupported. Nature never moves by jumps, but always in steady and supported advances. The implanting of a desire indicates that the gratification of that desire is in the constitution of the creature that feels it; the wish for food, the wish for motion, the wish for sleep, for society, for knowledge, are not random whims, but grounded in the structure of the creature, and meant to be satisfied by food, by motion, by sleep, by society, by knowledge. If there is the desire to live, and in larger sphere, with more knowledge and power, it is because life and knowledge and power are good for us, and we are the natural depositories of these gifts. . . . All I have seen teaches me to trust the Creator for all I have not seen. Whatever it be which the great Providence prepares for us, it must be something large and generous, and in the great style of his works. The future must be up to the style of our faculties, — of memory, of hope, of imagination, of reason" (*Letters and Social Aims,* pp. 319-321).

certain consolation from the sufferings in his life, he draws it from the hope regarding the enjoyment of the supreme good in the future life. If in the turbulent sea and the tempest of life's temptations man finds a calm harbor, he finds it through the compass of immortality, in which the supreme good is found. . . . If you deprive man of hope in the future enjoyment of the supreme good, man will become the unhappiest of all creatures, his life will become a moonless night. . . . He would pass his life sad and dejected, and in his despair he would put an end to his life. . . .[11] Thus the hope in the enjoyment of the supreme good, being a power of consolation, is divine and as such true. Hence, in hoping in the enjoyment of the supreme good, man believes that he has an immortal soul. God mystically informs man of this; and God's goodness, which is manifested everywhere, persuades him that he has an immortal soul.

### (viii) *Proof of the Immortality of the Soul from the Idea of the Immortality of the Soul in Us*

That man has an immortal soul is proved by the fact that he has the idea of the immortality of the soul innate in himself. Man receives his ideas from the surrounding world. Nature daily teaches him about the mortality of beings and their complete disappearance. Hence the idea of death and disappearance should be man's positive final conclusion. . . . Yet man has the idea of immortality, despite the images of death that reach his sight every day. How did he rise from the idea of death to the idea of immortality? How did he become convinced of this truth and build his whole way of life on it? An inference from death to immortality is impossible, and hence inadmissible. Man, then, did not receive the idea of immortality from nature. The idea of immortality exists in God, and God

---

[11] This view has been expressed by William James, too. "The bare assurance," he remarks, "that this natural order is not ultimate but a mere sign or vision, the external staging of a many-storied universe, in which spiritual forces have the last word and are eternal, is enough to make life seem worth living, in spite of every contrary presumption suggested by its circumstances on the natural plane. Destroy this inner assurance, however. . . and all the light and radiance of existence is extinguished at a stroke. Often enough the wild-eyed look at life — the suicidal mood — will then set in" (*The Will to Believe,* New York, 1897, pp. 56-57).

can impart the idea of immortality. . . . Hence man received the idea of immortality from the eternal God. Whatever being is capable of receiving something from God has the receptivity for this, and understands God and His divine revelation. Now man, not having received the idea of immortality from anywhere else, has received it and has it from God. Hence man has the receptivity, understands God, and has a spirit that communes with God Who reveals Himself. Therefore man is not soulless and mindless matter, but a being with soul and intellect, receptive of divine revelation. Such a being must have an immortal soul, inasmuch as he communes with God and is taught and made wise by Him with a view to his perfection, which without immortality is purposeless. Hence man has an immortal soul.

(ix) *Proof of the Immortality of the Soul from the Moral Pleasure that Develops in Us as We Practice Virtue*

He who practices virtue experiences a pleasure that is unknown to those who do not practice it — for instance, when he relieves those who are weighed down by want, when he comforts the unfortunate and makes the unhappy participants of his own happiness, when he has only two shirts and gives one to a person who is shivering from the winter cold. . . . The violation of justice arouses indignation and stirs up the virtuous man to defend justice. Here is a man struggling in behalf of justice, of truth, of freedom. He dies, and during his last moments he expresses the satisfaction which fills his heart that he is dying fighting for virtue. He is not concerned about himself, he is indifferent about his own life, he disregards death, and is concerned about the result of his struggle, whether he has won, whether justice has prevailed, whether truth has come to reign and falsehood has been crushed, whether tyranny has been abolished, whether freedom rules, whether the fetters of slavery have been shattered. How inexplicable is this feeling! It is an insoluble mystery without immortality. Only immortality can inspire immortal ideas, can inform the striver about the value of virtue. . . . Only immortality incites man to great sacrifices. It bids soldiers to die for the sake of their duty; it imposes self-denial upon those who pursue knowledge for the benefit of mankind; it gives rise to holy martyrs of societies; it consoles those who suffer for the sake of virtue; it rests the heart that has been disturbed by ingratitude; it incites the wealthy to distribute their wealth to the poor, and the poor to endure their poverty with moral calm; it gives courage to him who is mortally ill to await the arrival of death peacefully. Immortality, speaking mystically in the heart of man, incites man to all his noble deeds. . . .

Thus the moral pleasure that arises in the heart of man is occasioned by the immortality of the soul, which is in the image of God and consequently has the marks and eternity of the archetype. The soul, then, perceives that it is immortal, and for this reason it incites man to sacrifices for the sake of justice, truth, beauty, goodness, and perfection. For this reason, too, it gives the necessary courage for fulfilling its biddings, and rewards through moral pleasure, which it provides as the earnest of the supreme good which is reserved for man. Man, therefore, has been created for immortality.

### (x) *Proof of the Immortality of the Soul from the Idea of Eternity*

Man introduces the idea of the infinite in all the things that interest him. He seeks to extend his existence, and through all the available means he endeavors to succeed in the goal he aspires after. . . . His struggle on earth is directed to supporting his eternity. He wants and seeks through his inventions, through his achievements, to leave indelible traces of his passage. The idea of fame after death is his sweetest dream, which alleviates the pains from the efforts he makes for perpetuating the memory of his existence. Despite the fact that the changing nature of the things of the world loudly speaks of their transitory existence, man gives little attention to it and voluntarily turns a deaf ear to the re-echoing voice. He seeks to perpetuate, if not himself, at least his name. He does not acquiesce to disgrace. He thinks that he perpetuates his existence in his descendants. An inner voice persuades him to think that even after the end of his earthly life he will not disappear, but will exist somewhere, enjoying the satisfaction which the reward for his achievements on the earth would have provided him. He regards death, even though evident, as a powerless obstacle to his plans, wherefore he proceeds with his great undertakings, not taking it at all into consideration, but moving ahead more as an immortal than as a mortal. The more the preservation of his undertakings seems to extend beyond the grave, the more then enthuse him. A strange phenomenon: the grave and death, as if thin clouds, disperse before the brilliant ray of immortality.

Who does not see in this phenomenon the obvious revelation of the immortality of the soul? And how could this have been a common feeling of mankind, if it were not innate? How could it have been so strong, if there were no inner perception? How could God have implanted in our nature a feeling simultaneously so strong and so deceptive? If we deny the truth of the immortality of the soul, we must first deny man's nature. Without the idea of the existence of immortality, man is an inexplicable being. In order to explain him, we must admit the immortality of his soul. . . .

(xi) *Proof of the Immortality of the Soul from the Love of Beauty, Goodness, Truth, and Justice*

The love of abstract preoccupations is a psychical phenomenon that testifies to the existence of the soul, while the character of the objects with which the soul occupies itself declares its immortality. The innate bent towards philosophy, the desire to arrive at the perfect through the relatively perfect, the ineffable joy upon finding the truth, testify to man's spiritual nature and its character. The love of beauty, goodness, and truth is a ladder that leads man above the visible creation to another, spiritual world, whence it contemplates the wisdom of the Creator, understands His wonderful works, discerns His omnipotence, discovers everywhere His presence. God speaks to him face to face. How great a gift! How great a power! How great an honor and glory for earthly man! Now could God's wisdom have endowed man with such powers, if man perishes in the grave? What would their purpose have been? Of what benefit, if everything is lost after death?

How is it that, contrary to nature, dust delights in abstract ideas? How is it that physical man likes more to preoccupy himself with metaphysical than with physical inquiry? Whence this eros in matter for things spiritual? Where does this eros lurk? Where does joy go[12] — this divine spiritual ambrosia that vivifies the man who occupies himself with philosophy? What is the relationship between matter and spirit? Spirit as such can rejoice, because the discovery of a truth perfects it, lifts it up a step higher on the ladder of perfection. But why should matter rejoice? What benefit has matter derived, especially since it feels pain and distress the more such delights and spiritual pleasures increase in number and intensity? What joy does the body have when the spirit is intoxicated with the heavenly nectar? If man were only matter, why is not matter satisfied to wallow in itself, but seeks to elevate itself? If the grave and complete destruction await it, why does it sacrifice itself? And the strangest of all, why does God reveal Himself to it, if it is destined to lose completely its knowledge of Him?

Man searches to find the Creator of nature, its good Artist, the orderer of the universe, and to know Him from Whom he receives the idea of the beauty that pervades abundantly the whole world of creatures. The order, the harmony in all things, the wise arrangement and government of the universe, its wondrous beauty and radiant loveliness lift the mind of man to the First Cause, which created everything with wisdom; and they occasion the growth of the divine eros for philosophy and knowledge, through which he seeks to penetrate the depths of divine wisdom and to be initiated into the mysteries of the creation, through which [mysteries] all things were formed and are sustained. The study of things reveals the goodness of the Divine Creator and develops the feeling of love for the supreme Good, which attracts man towards itself. . . .

These psychical phenomena would have been entirely irreconcilable with the wisdom of God, if the grave were the termination of man's existence. But as this is contrary to the wisdom of God, it follows that man has a spirit receptive of the knowledge of

---

12 After death.

God and hence immortal; for the mortal is unworthy of such a value and honor,[13] inasmuch as it perishes. Therefore, man has an immortal soul, because where there is a knowledge of God there is immortality also.

### (xii) Proof of the Immortality of the Soul from the Voice of Conscience

Conscience is an unbribable judge, a keeper of the written law which God has inscribed in the heart of man. It was necessary that the law have a guard, and actions their judge. The coexistence of these two in man testifies to man's freedom, his responsibility for his actions, his relation to his legislator, and the immortality of his soul. For if man did not have an immortal soul, the law would have been superfluous, and conscience would have been importunate and unreasonable; and man's actions would have had no moral character, being merely natural activities. But that there exists a written law and a vigilant guard of it is testified firstly by the universal belief of mankind and secondly by the moral state of each man, who either does good or does evil, who either keeps the law or transgresses it. The keeper of the moral law is recognized by his character. His peace of soul and serenity of heart are reflected upon his serene countenance, as in a mirror, and his life is like a brook that flows quietly in a delightful plain. The expectation of future rewards is expressed by his works and actions. . . . The transgressor of the law is wholly disturbed by the incessant accusation of his conscience and presents a pitiful and horrible picture. Peace and serenity, these two doves, the symbols of virtue and goodness, have departed. Sullenness, dejection, weariness, despondency, and despair are painted on his infuriated and altered face with dark colors. He awaits punishment. Yet now we behold both of them descending into the grave, and on the tombstone of the wicked man are written dithyrambs and symbols of victory and triumphs, whereas on the unwrought tombstone of the good man is depicted a palm branch, and sometimes he is covered ingloriously and obscurely with mere earth, and the grave where the body of this spiri-

---

13 *Viz.* the knowledge of God.

tual athlete was buried remains unknown. Whence this antithesis? Where is justice? Was the righteous man cheated? Where is the reward he expected, for which he strove, and in which he believed with holy faith? Now he is gone and his tomb has covered him completely. Were his expectations empty? Did the voice of his conscience lead him astray? The wicked man, on the other hand, who was censured by his conscience, who boldly transgressed the moral law, passed his life with honors and glory, and has received a splendid tomb and enduring memorials of his glory. Was the fear and disturbance unreasonable, and the censure of conscience purposeless? No! The righteous man was not deceived; because having lived in accordance with the demands of the moral law, he lived in accordance with his destiny. The law was ordained in order that man may be able to maintain his relation to God, and be able to preserve, develop, and perfect himself. Hence he who keeps the law is not deceived, because he fulfills his destiny. But the transgressor of the law is not deceived either, because through the transgression of the law he wages war against the work of God, and bears heavy responsibilities, and is aware of his guilt — his conscience informs him. But why did not divine justice give to each one according to his works? Precisely for this reason, that man lives after death, and in the endless and eternal life the just will receive the reward for their labors, and the wicked the deserts for their wickedness.

The attribute of God's justice would have been an empty word, without meaning, if it did not give to each according to his works. But because God is just and loves justice, it follows that virtue is rewarded and wickedness is punished. But inasmuch as divine justice is not completely manifested here, it follows that in the future life, which awaits all, divine justice will be fulfilled. Conscience, therefore, is a clear proof of man's moral freedom and of the immortality of his soul. Concerning the conscience that has gone astray, it is sufficient to remark that it, too, testifies to the existence of conscience, with the sole difference that the man who has lost the knowledge of the truth has led astray his conscience, which nevertheless always censures the transgression of the law. Concerning hardened conscience, we say that this is accidental, a result of extreme wickedness. It does not disprove the general principle that conscience is an unbribable judge. And since a trial presupposes freedom, and freedom presupposes a rational being, it follows that man, who gives an account of his actions, is a rational and free being that has consciousness of his acts and is punished or rewarded for them. In any case, therefore, those who are not rewarded in this life will receive the compensation for their virtue in the future life, which is eternal and everlasting.

Paul, the Apostle of the Gentiles, describes the censure of conscience in his Epistle to the Romans (7: 15-23), not dogmatically, but psychologically, philosophically. Through sound arguments, he proves that the moral law is written in the heart of man, and that conscience was placed as the true judge of man's actions. Conscience always testifies whether an act is in accord with the law or contrary to the law; it supports truth, honors virtue, praises moral wisdom, and recognizes these as the only things that are good and pleasing to God and proper to a rational being. The voice of conscience echoes in the hearing of every man. No sensible person ever denied the existence of this voice, or its censure, or the warfare it arouses against the transgressor of the divine law, against the transgressor of principles and convictions. Conscience, therefore, is evidence of the written law within us, which God inscribed in the hearts of men for the perfection of their immortal souls.

### (xiii) *Proof of the Immortality of the Soul from the Inner Revelation of God*

Towards proving the immortality of the soul of man we bring the inner revelation of God, through which man is taught supernatural truths and learns what is conducive to his salvation and beneficial. Man often owes the salvation of his soul and life to this inner revelation of God. It delivers him from danger through mystical inspiration, and informs him while awake or asleep of events that are taking place far away, as well as of events that have not yet occurred; and it reveals to him the will of God. These verified events are so many pieces of evidence that support man's relation to God, man's high worth, God's providence for man, the spiritual nature of man and the immortality of his soul. Those who deny these truths deny themselves and the loftiness of their worth, the end and aim of their presence in the world, as well as whence they came and whither they are going. Wherefore they go through their life after the manner of the irrational animals and arrive at its termination fearful, and stand terrified before the open grave. How often such materialists, philosophizing before the grave, come to sounder thoughts and confess their error? How often they repudiate their whole past life as a result of the beliefs about the immortality of the soul which they form when they are near the point of death? This happens often, because those who are approaching the termination of their life here are closer to the other life.[14] The soul has already cast off a large part of its burden, and the bonds that hold it here on earth are being severed. The spirit has been freed from many vain preoccupations, and the mist of darkness that covered it has been lifted. The light of eternal life has entered and illuminated the darkened mind, which gazes dazzled at the heavenly brightness that has dawned, and seeks to search through it. Man meditates on the eternal life, and in this meditation he surrenders his spirit, fully convinced of the reality of that life. The eternal life already has been revealed to him.

### (xiv) *The Immortality of the Soul Proved from the Christian Life*

The Christian life has been regarded as the life that befits and is proper to man. But why? What is holiness? What is the holy life? What do these abstract notions mean? Might they not be words devoid of meaning? Might not mankind have erred in its respect for the moral law? Might not false ideas about the laws of life, about itself, about its destiny have led it to absurd and erroneous principles, through which life was distinguished into the holy and the unholy, the saintly and the abominable?

But how did the error spread throughout the world? How is it that the whole of mankind, all the races on the earth and all the languages have words signifying such ideas? How is it that even the savages profess virtue as a fundamental doctrine of their reli-

---

[14] Cf. above, pp. 53-54.

## Proofs of Immortality

gions? Examine all the oldest religions of all the continents, go about the entire earth, search into the interior of Africa and the depths of America, enter into the lands of the savages, visit the islands of the oceans, study from a close distance the fundamental principles of the religions of the remotest countries, which have been separated by long distances, and you will ascertain that they all honor the holy and saintly life, and that all profess that only those who have led a holy life are enviable, dear to God and happy. . . .

Could the common opinion of mankind have erred? But it is impossible for everybody together to be mistaken. Hence common opinion is the true judge that safely judges about the value or lack of value of a thing. What it approves of is truly good, and what it disapproves of is truly bad[15]. . . . Consequently the holy life is the power that perfects man and renders him the most splendid, most beautiful, and noblest creature on earth.

But to what end this self-perfecting, these efforts, if the same fate is reserved for both the perfect and the imperfect? To what end, if the cold slab of the tomb will cover both completely, and the personality of him who strove for perfection will disappear together with the disintegration of his body? Why did the all-wise creative power place in man the power of self-perfection, so that through efforts, labors, and sacrifices he might become more splendid, if this perfection is to no end? But the wisdom of God excludes purposelessness. What then is the purpose? Here is a question that requires study and great attention. Let us see then what is the purpose of man's perfection through the virtuous and holy life.

The purpose of perfection through the moral and virtuous life, being a work of the divine will and wisdom, must be sublime, great, and divine, worthy of the divine will. The perfection and holiness of man that is sought is his deification (*apotheōsis*);[16] for

---

[15] Cf. Aristotle: "Those who deny that that which all creatures seek to obtain is good, are surely talking nonsense. For what all think to be good, that, we assert is good; and he that subverts our belief in the opinion of all mankind will hardly persuade us to believe his own either" (*Nichomachean Ethics*, Bk. X, Ch. 2).

[16] The Greek Church Fathers of the Byzantine period, as well as those before and after it, frequently speak of *theosis* or *apotheosis,* and quote Scrip-

God alone is perfect and holy. The purpose, therefore, of man's striving for perfection through the moral and holy life is the deification of man. God, then, has sought to render man a god, and this is the reason why He placed within him the power of development and the eros for perfection, for which man labors and struggles. The mystical voice of God that speaks in the heart of man strengthens him in this struggle, of which God is the judge, Who invisibly guides and supports him, utters words of life in his heart and leads him to the end for which man was created. This is the reason why neither the world with all its enjoyments and pleasures, nor glory, nor the splendor and pride of life can prevail over one who is struggling for virtue and the holy life. The voice which speaks mystically in the heart of man is so clear and distinct that it is understood as much by the civilized as by the savages. This voice renders the fallen cannibals human and it, too, preserves in man the characteristics that distinguish him from the irrational animals and the highest apes. Hence man was not created in order to perish, but in order to become a partaker of God's goodness and blessedness. Therefore man has an immortal soul.

(xv) *Religious Proof of the Immortality of the Soul*

Religion testifies to the immortality of the soul, because religion is an innate disposition of man towards spiritual communion with the absolute spirit of God. . . . The human spirit instinctively moves in pursuit of the absolute Spirit, and spontaneously rises towards the absolute Spirit. When the human spirit sets out to know the objects surrounding it, it does not stop anywhere, does not rest anywhere, but always moves and always seeks new knowledge. It strives to rise to the absolute Spirit, in which it believes it will find the rest which it is seeking. This phenomenon is something universal, being found in all the peoples and races on earth. There has been no people without religion; there has been no people

---

ture in connection ,with it. An often referred to passage is Psalm 81 (82): 6: "I have said, You are gods, and all of you sons of the Most High." Another passage which they frequently quote is 2 Peter 1: 4: ". . . That you might be partakers of the divine nature." *Theosis* means union with God, participation in God's perfection and blessedness.

## Proofs of Immortality

without worship of the Deity. Religion and the worship of the Deity testify to the innate impulse of the human spirit to seek the Deity. The denial of this truth is a denial of man's spiritual nature. To him who denies it we have nothing to say, because he has already denied himself, has denied his spiritual activity, has denied the longings of his spirit, the longings of his soul. We are addressing ourselves to him who admits his spiritual nature, the innate impulse of his spirit in quest of the Deity, the innate assiduity of his soul towards rising above the earthly and resting in the absolute Spirit. Religion testifies to the immortality of the soul, because religion is a result of man's inward perception of the communion of his spirit with the absolute Spirit. Religion has been the necessary consequence of God's communion with man and man's communion with God.

Furthermore, religion is the logical conclusion of the assiduity of the human spirit in its quest of the absolute Spirit; because the spirit that seeks the absolute Divine Spirit cannot be striving for the void, cannot be in error. It strives for and rises to the absolute Spirit, because it has been assured of the existence of the absolute Spirit, because it feels its kinship with the Spirit. The human spirit feels its immortality and strives for the Immortal. Now a spirit that seeks the immortal cannot be mortal. Immortality presses on towards immortality. The impetus of the spirit testifies to its immortal nature. Being a result of the communion of the human spirit with the Divine Spirit, religion testifies to the immortality of the soul.

This truth is also evinced by the religious virtues[17] that develop in the heart of the religious man. These virtues appear in all splendor and grace in revealed religion. This phenomenon testifies to the true communion of God with man, and the action of God on the soul of man. The religious virtues of the Christian are splendid evidence of God's communion with man; and God's communion with man and the imparting of the divine gifts testifies to the im-

---

[17] Nectarios divides the virtues into the religious and the moral. The religious virtues are faith, hope, and love. Both kinds of virtue are treated in detail in his book *Self-Knowledge*.

mortality of the soul. Thus religion testifies to the immortality of the soul of man.

(xvi) *The Immortality of the Soul Testified by the Innate Impulse to Worship God*

Another strange and quite inexplicable phenomenon for materialistic theories is the worship of the Deity. What is this phenomenon? What is this desire for the unkown? What is this inclination, yearning, and often eros for the Deity? Why do the mind and heart seek to leave the material and rise towards the heavenly, in order to worship the Deity and show their devotion to it? What is this tendency to withdraw from the body, to isolate that other entity in us that distinguishes itself from the body through its selfhood? What is this entity that calls itself the *I* (*ego*), that seeks to detach itself from the bonds of the body, in order to devote itself freely to preoccupation with wholly abstract objects, with the contemplation of things foreign to surrounding nature? How is it that material man likes to concern himself with abstract ideas? What are these abstract ideas? Here is a devout person who has renounced the world and the things of the world, in order to devote himself to the service of a certain invisible Being, and who submits himself to the absolute will of this Being. Why this dependence? What has prompted him thus to subjugate his own will? Behold this man before a floweret lauding its Artist. Its beauty engenders in his heart the feeling of worship, which accents his song in praise of his Creator. His lips sing to invisible nature, his tongue chants hymns of praise to the invisible Power, his heart rejoices and his spirit delights in this worship. He believes he has fulfilled his duty, which was imposed upon him by a certain mystical voice that he had to obey. And through this fulfillment he goes away full of gratification.

But having moved on a little, new objects at once present themselves to his sight, new feelings arise in his heart, and his tongue readily chants hymns of praise to the wonderful works of the Designer's marvellous wisdom. Each pace reveals works of art; each glance discovers masterpeices; and each work of art and masterpiece demands a singing of hymns. The wisdom, the goodness, and the providence that are emphatically manifested in all provoke the spectator to abandon the created world and rise to its Creator. . . .

This man walks on the earth, but his spirit is present in unknown realms. . . . His whole life is a series of apostasies from the earthly world. His food is the food of the Spirit. His delight is to meditate on the mighty works of God. The hymnody of his lips is a perpetually flowing fount. His heart is a place of sanctification for the dwelling of the Divine Creator. Although he lives on earth, he is foreign to it. His senses, like noble ministers of the spirit, serve his lofty will; they work in order to provide new occasions for glorifying the Creator. All through his life he has sought to approach the wise Designer, Whom he has loved with all his soul and heart and intellect, and towards Whom he has hastened every day. Is it possible for such a person not to have known Him? Is it possible for him to have loved the void, nonbeing? How did nonbeing reveal itself as Being? How did it reveal itself in the heart of the worshipper? O! impossible! The Creative Power that sustains all things is an existent Being, which always is and always will be; it is God, Who has created all things with wisdom, God Who reveals Himself in the world, God the beauty of Whose attributes attracts man and detaches him from the material world, in order to render him a dweller in the mansions of eternal blessedness.

Thus worship is man's true elevation. It is a true uplifting power, a true ladder that leads from earth to heaven; it leads as far as the eternal life. It ennobles and sanctifies man and renders him a likeness of God. Worship perfects man and renders him a son of God, according to the statement: "I have said: You are gods, and all of you sons of the Most High."[18] Now is it possible for such a man to die like the rest of the animals and to perish completely, to be annihiliated? Never, never! Man must have and has an immortal soul.

(xvii) *The Immortality of the Soul Testified by Man's Cognitive Nature*

Man is born a lover of knowledge, a lover of knowing.[19] Now

---

[18] Psalm 81 (82): 6.

what is this eros for knowledge? What is this aspiration after knowing? What is it that man desires and seeks to enjoy? Behold! everything before his eyes is invested with the garment of beauty and order. Their representations are very good. All things are endowed with so many attractive qualities that they provide delight, pleasure, satisfaction to all, and fulfill and satisfy the demands of all. How satisfied man ought to be! What an abundance of blessings! Yes, all things are abundantly diffused, yet man seeks and desires to know.[20]

It is a strange desire. Whence was it born in him? It is quite impossible to explain it without admitting a rational power in man, conjoined with spiritual powers and impelling man to pursue knowledge. The inclination to know is a demand of a rational soul, which delights not in an abundance of enjoyments, but in finding the reason for the creation of each creature and the discovery of the laws of their preservation. The soul seeks the wisdom of the Creator in the creation. It seeks to acquaint itself with, and enter into, the depths of the Creative Spirit. It seeks to know all things and to encompass them in the mind. It seeks to render itself like God. . . .

In which species of animals is such a phenomenon observed? What animal abandoned the things of sense and turned to the search of things that are above sense? Which epoch throughout the centuries pointed to even a single such example? How, then, having such testimonies of man's supersensible delight do we not rise to that spiritual world, in order to find there man's true character,

---

[19] Cf. Aristotle: "All men by nature desire to know. An indication of this is the delight we take in our senses; for apart from their use we love them for themselves, and most of all the sense of sight. Not only with a view of action, but even when no action is contemplated, we prefer sight to practically all the other senses. The reason is that of all the senses sight best helps us to know things" (*Metaphysics,* Bk. I, 980a).

[20] Man's search for philosophical knowledge, for wisdom, does not arise from physical want, from the struggle for physical survival. On the contrary, it presupposes the satisfaction of material wants. Thus Aristotle remarks: "When all such inventions [those directed to the necessities of life or to recreation] were already established, the branches of knowledge which do not aim at giving pleasure or at the necessities of life were discovered, and first in the places where men first began to have leisure" (*Metaphysics,* Bk. I, 981b).

which has nothing in common with the sensible world? O! indeed, the knowledge of truth is an attribute not of matter, but of spirit. Man is a spiritual rather than a material being, wherefore he delights more in spiritual than in material things. Now is it possible for spirit, which has received such longings, which thus rises up towards God, which seeks Him in all things, which is perfected by its knowledge of Him, to be a part of matter and to return to it at death? No! a myriad times no! The acceptance of such an idea is an insult to truth, is an insult to spirit. No, the soul is not matter, is not a secretion of the brain,[21] but is a special creature of God, made to image the Creator on earth and to live eternally in the world of spirits. Yes, man was created for immortality.[22]

(xviii) *The Immortality of the Soul Testified by the Social Life of Man*

Social life is a very strong proof of the immortality of the human soul.... The wonders of art and knowledge of all the ages, which evoke the astonishment and admiration of everybody, are due to the social life of man. Society provided man with all the means for his development. It has been the mother of his first ideas. As a faithful depository, it has safeguarded all the productions of the spirit, all the arts and sciences, and has handed down to later generations the whole spiritual wealth of Antiquity. Social life has made possible the prosperity and happiness of man and has insured their preservation, development, and progress. Thus society is a very great good, the horn of Amalthea, the inexhaustible source of blessings, and the provider of every benefaction.

But what is the connecting bond of societies? What is the firm

---

[21] St. Nectarios is alluding to the dictum of the French physician and philosopher Cabanis (1757-1808) that the brain secretes thought as the liver secretes bile.

[22] The argument of St. Nectarios as presented in this paragraph has a close parallel in the following one by St. Athanasius: "This is the reason why the soul thinks of and bears in mind things immortal and eternal, namely, because it is itself immortal. And just as, the body being mortal, its senses also have mortal things as their objects, so, since the soul contemplates and beholds immortal things, it follows that it is immortal and lives for ever" (*A Select Library of Nicene and Post-Nicene Fathers,* Second Series, Vol. IV, p. 22).

rock on which they are founded? What is the power that has rendered man social? Did a simple innate tendency, as in those animals that unite in herds, give rise to the first societies? But then why did not man's rationality dissolve them? This power of objectifying what is external to him, engenders myriads of errors and drives man to acts of violence against his fellow men. The idea that it was common interest that led men to form the first societies is a hypothesis which has, indeed, probability, but does not account for their preservation; it expresses the necessity of the social life, but is silent as regards the means of its perpetuation. Reciprocity of interests is not a strong enough bond for the preservation of societies, because greed and the other passions are able to give birth to deception, to guile, and to secret betrayal of the covenant. And the stronger might oppress and exterminate the weaker and paralyze society. Hence mutual interest is not a sufficiently strong means of sustaining the common bond of societies. Societies are sustained and perpetuated by moral laws. If moral law did not exist, societies would not have been preserved. Moral law, therefore, is and has been the bond that keeps societies united. Wherefore moral law is the necessary condition for the formation of societies of men, because it alone conduces to the foundation of society and to the progress and prosperity of men.

And if progress, happiness, and development are products of society, without which they are not secured, and these are the only necessary means for the perfection of man, it follows that without society the development, progress, and perfection of man are impossible, and that society and the social life are an inseparable necessity of human life. But since society cannot stand without moral life, unavoidable necessity imposes the moral life upon man, in order that society might be sustained and through it man might be developed and perfected and live happily. . . .

But morality and perfection through society are incomprehensible and superfluous notions for a being that is annihilated. Everything in nature is purposive, because the Divine Creator made everything with wisdom. Is it then possible that morality and self-perfection are purposeless? But if everything purposive has necessary existence for a certain reason of the Divine Will, what is the reason for man's ethical perfection? If we view him as a purely material being, whose existence ends at the grave, then virtue and perfection are barren suffering and vain display; and the price paid for these at the expense of the welfare of the body is much greater than the advantages obtained. But is it possible that the ethical perfection of a being be pursued at the heavy expense of the body, only to disappear in the grave? No! a thousand times no! because it is contrary to the wisdom and justice of God. . . . Therefore, as a social and ethical being man has an immortal soul.

Those who deny the immortality of the soul undermine both the moral law and the foundations of societies, which they want to see collapsing into ruins, in order that they might prove that man is an ape, from which they boast that they are descended. Fortunately, however, societies have always repelled these destructive ideas with aversion, and have opposed to them their moral strength and the moral consciousness of their ancestral nobility. Materialistic ideas have always corrupted societies, whereas ethical and psychological[23] ideas have always benefited them. The history of all the nations bears witness to this truth. Let us look at the history of ancient Greece. Greece has been the fatherland of philosophy. Now who among the philosophers benefited Greece? Whose philosophical principles elevated her? And whose philosophical ideas debased and corrupted the citizens? Behold Socrates, Plato, Aristotle, and Plutarch and the other workers of noble philosophy. What century will ever forget them? Who does not admire the age when they lived as one of glory and grandeur? But behold also the company of the Epicureans. What kind of men were Diagoras, Aristippus, Hegesias and their likes, the co-workers of ancient wretchedness? What were their deeds? History has written black pages about them. What would have happened if the ideas of such philosophers had gained general acceptance? Who can now accept as sound and true ideas and principles that destroyed the bases of social life? Who can espouse views that are opposed to the very happiness and well-being of man, views which destroy all that is beautiful, good,

---

[23] The term *psychological* is used here in its strict, etymological sense, to signify ideas pertaining to the *psyche* or soul, viewed as an entity distinct from the material organism, the body.

noble, sublime, admirable, precious, divine, and build upon the ruins all that is ugly, evil, ignoble, base, abominable, mean, satanic? Who can consent to believe that this disorderly life is the life that is proper to man? Nobody! Because man is conscious of his nobility, even when he does not know his origin.

# V

## I. N. THEODORAKOPOULOS

(1900 —)

Ioannis Theodorakopoulos

# BIOGRAPHICAL NOTE ON THEODORAKOPOULOS

Ioannis N. Theodorakopoulos, the leading philosopher of Greece today, was born on February 28, 1900, at Sparta. He was educated at the Rizarios School (1915-1920), and at the universities of Vienna (1922-1923) and Heidelberg (1923-1925), where he studied philosophy and philology. He took the Ph.D. degree at the University of Heidelberg. In 1930 he was appointed instructor in philosophy at the University of Thessaloniki; and in 1933, professor of philosophy at the same university. Since 1939 he has been professor of philosophy at the University of Athens. In 1954 he was invited by the State Department to visit the United States. During his visit here he attended many philosophical meetings and was awarded an honorary Doctor of Laws degree by the University of Ohio. In 1958 he was invited to western Germany and lectured at various universities there. In 1960 he was elected member of the Academy of Athens, Greece's highest cultural institution. He served as president of the Academy during 1963-1964.

The following books are his principal philosophical writings:

(1) *Platons Dialektik des Seins,* Tubingen, 1927.

(2) *Plotins Metaphysik des Seins,* Buhl/Baden, 1928.

(3) *Eisagōgē ston Platōna* ("Introduction to Plato"), Athens, 1940, 1947, 1958, 1964.

(4) *Systēma Philosophikēs Ethikēs* ("System of Philosophical Ethics"), Vol. I, Athens, 1947, 1952, 1960.

(5) *Platōnos Phaidros* ("Plato's Phaedrus")—ancient Greek text with modern Greek translation, introduction, and notes—, Athens, 1948.

(6) *Christianika kai Philosophika Meletēmata* ("Christian and Philosophical Studies"), Athens, 1949.

(7) *Ho Faust tou Gaite* ("Goethe's Faust")—modern Greek translation, aesthetic and philosophical interpretation—, Athens, 1956, 1963.

(8) *Platōn-Plōtinos-Origenēs* ("Plato - Plotinus - Origen") Athens, 1959.

Many of the briefer philosophical writings of Theodorakopoulos have appeared in the *Archeion Philosophias kai Theōrias tōn Epistēmōn* ("Archives of Philosophy and Theory of the Sciences"), a quarterly which he took the initiative in founding and of which he was the editor from 1929, when it began to be published, to 1940, when the last issues appeared.

Like the other thinkers presented in this book, Theodorakopoulos does not follow some one philosopher or school of philosophy. He assimilates into his own thought elements drawn from many philosophers. The most outstanding influences in his philosophy are Socrates, Plato, and Plotinus. But philosophy for Theodorakopoulos, although an extremely valuable discipline for discovering the nature of man, the purpose of human life, and the means of attaining it, does not provide the ultimate solution to the problem of man as a concrete being, as a personality with a yearning for immortality, for perfection, for salvation. This solution is to be sought, he holds, beyond the realm of reason, of philosophic thought, in the realm of faith, of authentic Christianity.

# *Theodorakopoulos*

## CONCERNING THE SOUL[1]

### 1

Each man knows himself as a psychical being, lives his life and is conscious of it as a psychical reality. This means that each man distinguishes himself as a psychical interiority from everything else that is around him; that each man distinguishes his psychical presence from his bodily reality. His inner presence is constituted of experiences immediately accessible only to him. This direct knowledge or acquaintance of each man with his psychical reality constitutes the interior self-affirmation of his being, of the fact that he exists. What he feels and is conscious of, what he yearns for and plans, what he wants and thinks about, all these are immediate data and constitute his interiority; they are closer to his self than everything else.

But this direct knowledge of man as regards his psychical events and experiences, this direct consciousness which he has of his being and his interior, this self-affirmation of his psychical presence, is not identical with the science of the soul. It is only an indispensible presupposition for one's proceeding deeper and grasping the notion of the soul, that is, for acquiring a full knowledge concerning the being of the soul. The acquaintance that each man

---

[1] From the book *Christianika kai Philosophika Meletemata,* Athens, 1949, pp. 57-72.

has of his psychical reality is a consciousness, a self-affirmation without reasoning, whereas systematized knowledge or science is also understanding. If the first acquaintance is immediate, the second, knowledge and understanding, is mediate. This mediate understanding is the science of the soul.

The first condition for going beyond self-affirmation to a mediate understanding of our self is to distinguish psychical from bodily reality, to distinguish the soul clearly from the body and to view the soul as an incorporeal unity. This strict distinction is indispensible; otherwise it is impossible for us to form an objective notion of the soul. What we feel and are conscious of, what we live immediately in psychical reality, we must grasp with our mind also, with pure understanding, as a unity qualitatively different from mere corporeality; otherwise we come to an impass, and discussion about the soul is vain. If we do not distinguish the soul qualitatively from the body and do not grasp it as a unity, there is no science of the soul, no psychology. A psychology without a soul is idle talk, plain vanity.

Whatever is a body has extension, weight, and all the related marks of corporeality. The incorporeal has none of these attributes. Even the simplest psychical events — sensations — are qualitatively different from bodily and physiological functions or activities. Sensations are psychical, that is, they have no bodily or physiological attribute. They are experiences of the soul, perceptive states; and these have neither extension nor weight nor any other material attribute. Sensations are a kind of acquaintance which the soul has with objects.

When we say that the incorporeal has no attribute of the corporeal, we mean precisely this, that it is different in kind, a different world. Although the soul is joined to the body and functions together with the body, nevertheless it is not corporeal. The body is an object of the senses, whereas the soul is never accessible to the senses. The soul is a separate unity, quite different from the body. Plato was the first to distinguish the soul from the body with logical rigor; and said that "the soul must necessarily be ungenerated and immortal" (*Phaedrus,* 246a), and that the "soul is altogether different from the body" (*Laws,* XII, 959a). Elsewhere again he defines the soul as the principle and source of all the manifestations of the psychical world.

So if we want now to define the soul more positively, we must say that the soul is the principle of another world, of the world which is not seen, but which we live with absolute certainty; because the certainty that we have about our psychical events, in which we exist and live, is one that we do not have about the events around us. In all the psychical events there is the soul, as a principle, as a single and unique entity. And when a psychical event has passed, the soul which sustains it abides, abides as a consciousness of that event, as the principle which lived it.

But while the soul is together with all the psychical events and experiences, it is not identical with them; the psychical events and the soul are distinct. Hence we must not only distinguish the soul from the body, but must proceed to a second distinction: we must distinguish the soul as an indestructible unity, as a substance and a presence of the spirit, from everything which it lives, that is, from psychical events and experiences. A psychical event is what it is, that is, is different from other psychical events, is not identical with them, it differs from them. But while the soul is something other than all the psychical events and experiences, it is always in all of them. It has presence in all; without it they are incomprehensible and nonexistent. The flux of the psychical world, of psychical events, is not also a flux of the soul: the soul remains the same in the midst of all the events that flow and change. In the midst of the incessant becoming of the psychical world, there exists the soul as a center of reference, as a principle and presence. And when the psychical events are not present, when they have passed, it is still present. The unabated, therefore, principle in all psychical events is the soul. And because it is the cognitive principle, knows other things, events, and has consciousness, we can say that the soul is an unabated wakefulness, is that which is aware of other things and of itself. All other things move within it, exist for a while and then do not, whereas it exists always, is in all of them, without passing away as they do.

Now although the soul is always the stable principle of the inner world, it is nevertheless something that moves, that moves it-

---

2  The ethical.

self. But this motion (*kinēsis*) is not a change of place, is not material, but mental. It is not a movement from one place to another, but is a movement of the spirit from one thought to another, from one psychical event to another. The soul moves of itself. This means that it apprehends both itself and other things. Also the movement of the soul means that the soul sees what it is as it proceeds from one thought to another, from one experience to another. This movement of the soul is its life. When we say here life, we do not mean animal reality, the vital functions; we always mean consciousness, that is, the knowledge the soul has of its being, which is one and indivisible, and of the being of its experiences. Thus the soul is the unity of consciousness and of being. . . .

However, the whole inner world of the soul is not given to it from the beginning, is not ready at the outset, but develops with it as the soul is educated, that is, as it proceeds from a state of immediate experience and acquaintance to mediate knowledge and understanding. This movement of the soul from immediate experience and acquaintance to mediate understanding and knowledge, from simple experience to consciousness and self-consciousness is called education. Education is the conscious movement of the soul from the immediately given to mediate concepts. The soul, then, is not ready and developed from the beginning, but has to develop itself in the midst of concepts, feelings, and all the other activities. . . .

Self-development in the case of the soul means something infinitely different from what it means in the case of the plant and the rest of animate nature. The limits of the form of the plant or the animal are restricted and the type is given in advance, is ready, whereas in the case of the soul its inner, spiritual development is unlimited, and its endless progress depends on its self-consciousness. The development of this infinite potentiality, which is called the soul, is the work and purpose of the life of the soul. Aristotle distinguishes the *potential being* of the soul from its *actual being*, and it is through this distinction that he understands psychical reality. Potential being signifies the infinite potentiality of the soul, while actual being signifies the reality of the soul. The movement of the soul is effected by the passage from potentiality to actuality, from possibility to reality. I am potentially rational when

I am still intellectually immature; I am actually rational when I have become mature, when the possibility has become a reality.

What is especially significant, however, is this: that as the soul moves from potential towards actual being, from possibility towards reality, from its unmanifested towards its manifested essence, it becomes simultaneously conscious of its responsibility. As it moves from the one state towards the other, it becomes conscious of its freedom. In the case of the plant and the animal, too, there is a movement from potentiality towards actuality, from possibility towards reality; but this movement is automatic. The movement of the soul, however, from potentiality towards actuality is self-conscious: the soul itself opens its way and lives with the consciousness of responsibility.

During this conscious movement of the soul from potentiality towards actuality, there open up within the soul the basic paths of its being: sensation, imagination, representation, understanding, will, feeling. All these are basic modes according to which the soul moves from potentiality towards actuality. The soul, both as substance and as actuality, is manifested in these, and renders its being conscious in these. The paths which the soul opens with its basic powers, and through which it becomes real as actuality, are the cognitive, the practical,[2] the aesthetic, and the religious.

The soul is cognitive, that is, it knows both what happens within itself and what happens around it. . . . Our knowledge is a two-fold relation: it is a logical relation to objects and a logical relation to ourselves, to our cognitive principle, the purely rational soul. Through knowledge we go far beyond mere sensation; we overcome the immediate data of the senses and acquire a high degree of freedom in relation to things. This freedom which knowledge gives was the reason why Plato characterized knowledge as a kind of immortality of man. Insofar as man thinks and knows, he is not mortal, but partakes of immortality. Through knowledge he advances beyond his simple animal and mortal presence, is freed, becomes a pure soul.

But knowledge, regardless how much power it might give to man, is in itself limited, because none of its achievements is final,

---

[2] The ethical.

or leads to the absolute. Every point of knowledge is only a stage from which the soul must move further ahead; it is never a terminus. Only a conceited soul can boast that its knowledge has reached the absolute. But this arrogance is not reconcilable with the character of real science. . . .

The value and efficacy of the cognitive way and all the other ways cannot be appreciated unless the soul is viewed as something personal, as a personality. The soul as a self is chiefly a person. The notion of the person contains in itself the notion of the ego, that is, of the unique rational monad; and this in turn contains in itself the idea of freedom. Men have personality because they are rational, because they have spirituality. Hence personality is never something external, but is something *par excellence* inner. I have personality means that I as a definite spiritual monad have an absolute relation to myself, and that in the midst of all finite things, in the midst of all objects, return freely to my own being. . . .

The soul, therefore, is not a blind power, but is chiefly a personal consciousness. It knows itself as a spirit and has personal responsibility for itself. As a personality, the soul is unique and unrepeatable; that is, it has an eternal foundation and cannot be referred to other things, such as the elements or blind life. Hence, as a soul or spirit, as a person or self, man is an irreplaceable value. Each one is, in relation to another, unique and irreplaceable. Each one is an eternal point of responsibility and freedom.

Thus what we call personality is not composed of other things, nor is it a result of external causes. The soul finds itself as a unique presence, as a unique existent. Through its basic ways — the cognitive, the practical, the aesthetic, and the religious — it opens paths within itself and constructs intellectual worlds. The boundaries of these worlds never coincide with those of the sensible world: these worlds of the spirit are altogether different. Thus physical reality, which is revealed to us by our senses, is one thing, and the world of the spirit, which is accessible to the understanding and to the inner consciousness of the soul, is something else. The secret of the personality, therefore, is that its boundaries do not coincide either with those of palpable life or with those of physical reality. Even the soul of the child, through the imagination, goes beyond mere physical reality, beyond what we usually call the environment. The environment is much narrower than the inner world of the imagination, which fills the soul of the child. Indeed, we should not speak of environment when we are discussing man, because man as a spiritual presence lives in another world, much more extensive than the world of phenomena. Animals and plants have their environment and live and remain within it, whereas man has not an environment but a world. . . .

When we say that the soul is a person, an existence, we do not mean only its cognitive capacity, its rationality, but also its moral character. The self of man has not only cognitive freedom, but also ethical freedom; that is, it is specified by its ethical quality, by ethical characteristics. The soul is human not only because it has the power of distinguishing moral values both positively and negatively, but also because it has will, the power of performing and positing moral actions. And first of all it posits itself as a moral work, as a moral monad. This would have been impossible if it did not possess freedom. The essence of spirit, of the soul, is freedom. Now as the soul posits itself as an ethical personality and an intrinsic value, as it acts ethically and grasps its inner quality as freedom, it communes with itself. In this communion with itself, it becomes conscious of its unique dignity, becomes conscious of its freedom, and through this it understands its humanity. It sees within itself the essence of man.

The soul is *par excellence* social, that is, it communes with itself, returns with its freedom and apprehends its own being; and at the same time it communes with others . Thus the soul becomes moral as it returns to itself and as it communes with the other, the neighbor. As it sees itself, it sees the other; as it sees within itself the dignity of man, so it sees within the other, the neighbor, the same dignity. Just as through knowledge the soul opens a relation, a communion with other entities, with objects, so through its moral self-consciousness it opens a relation with itself and with others. Thus the human soul is not an absolutely isolated monad, but is social, is a member of a spiritual republic, of a world whose centers are as many as are the persons. These centers, these persons, tend to commune with each other, and thus to receive each other's law within themselves. This is ethical communion. Within it men are centers of one spirit and one system of values.

But in general also the soul is social, that is, it tends by nature to associate with what is about it. Converse is the law of the soul. Thus the soul communes with the universe. This communion takes place in many ways: through the imagination, through knowledge, through feeling, through conscience. A soul which did not have the power of associating either through knowledge, or through feeling, or through any of its other powers would not have been just what the soul is by its essence. Hence knowledge as well as action and imagination and feeling — all four of these basic functions — relate the soul, bring it into association. On the other hand, during this association all these basic activities are manifested in their fullness.

Thus during its ethical communion with other souls, the soul manifests itself and is self-acting. Without this self-action and self-manifestation, without this communion with itself and with others, the soul's essence is not fully realized. During this communion the soul gives and takes. And as it gives and takes it grows, that is, it actualizes its essence. Thus its whole life is a dialogue with itself and with others. It is precisely this that Plato saw and represented in a most classical manner. The dialogue is for Plato the basic instrument of expressing the life of the soul, because the whole life of the soul is a communion and dialogue. Through knowledge, action, and art the soul communes with other souls and with objects.

However, beyond these kinds of communion, beyond this rational, moral, and aesthetic dialogue these exists something else still deeper. That is, the soul is also a religious existence, a religious personality. This means that the soul opens within itself a higher kind of dialogue; it begins a communion with the highest Being, the source of all things. Through its knowledge, its acts, and its art the soul never reaches the end: all these are interminable. But as a spiritual and personal monad, the soul longs for the goal, for the termination. Besides, it feels that, although it is the source of these paths which have no terminus, although it is the starting point of this whole cognitive, ethical, and aesthetic striving, it does not create itself. As it follows its life and its being, as it seeks to find its first cause, its origin, the only thing it achieves is to be led more and more to its depths. Here it sees that its life and being gush up unceasingly without its own efficacy. Its life and being within do not cease. No matter how much it turns inwardly, it always finds itself as being and as activity. Now whatever finds itself without being the cause of itself, whatever is conscious of its being without creating itself, such an entity is not a creator but a creature. Thus the soul is now conscious of itself as a creature. It is aware that it does not create itself, but finds itself created. What it achieves through its knowledge and other activities is chiefly this: to bring to light the inner content which it finds, to develop the world of the spirit. And as it develops within this world, which it itself develops, it understands that this world has no boundaries. But its aspiration is to reach the end; and because this is unachievable, it returns to itself hoping to find here the root of its being. But here, too, within itself, it finds an incessant gushing up of life without beginning. The more it intensifies this return to itself, the more it gathers itself within itself, the more it repents after its achievements in the sphere of the spirit, the more it becomes conscious that it is a creature, and the more it returns inside itself. This repentance and consciousness that it is a creature engender its religious experience.

In this state it lives humbled, it sees itself and all other things as creatures, it yearns for its eternal source, it burns with the eros to return not only to itself, but to its source. With this feeling the soul sinks into all things, not in order to remain within them, but in order in this manner to pass beyond these things which are creatures and unite itself with the root of all things, the principle of the universe.

Through this repentance and humility the soul loses neither its unity, nor its uniqueness, nor its personality, but becomes aware that there exists something else which is higher, and in which these personal centers of the spirit find rest. The separation and difference, the division in general which distinguishes the world of creatures, is eliminated in this divine unity, without the soul being abolished as a personal presence of the spirit. Man now knows himself "in God," whereas previously he knew himself in his own spirit or in the world. This means that man now finds rest, whereas before he was struggling.[3] The satisfaction which he had from his works was relative; the satisfaction he now has is absolute. Now he feels that he is saved, for he returns not only to himself, but also to his source. This does not mean, however, that man becomes God: man remains man, that is, a distinct personal monad of spirit. Man only communes with God, rests in God.

Christianity developed fully this free and self-active relation of man to the Deity, of the finite to the infinite. This means that it grasped in all its depth the relation of the particular to the universal, of the creature to the Creator; and conversely, the relation of the Creator to the creature. There is no deeper relation of the Creator to the creature than this: that the Creator should suffer for the sake of His creature, that He should put on the body of man and die for the sake of His creature.

2

What we have said thus far had as its purpose only to give an image of the soul, to exhibit the soul as a rational unity, as a personal presence, as a spiritual existence. The soul is a personal presence of a spirit with an eternal root. However, this fact about the soul, its uniqueness and irreplaceable value, is obscured today more than ever before by various conceptions — by social systems [4] and by purely intellectual systems.[5] All these have the character of abstractness, that is, they withdraw from the soul as a personal presence, from the concrete being and personality that is called the soul. Whereas the philosophical teachings of Classical Greek Antiquity never forget their source, that is, the soul as a personality, today's conceptions and slogans, be they social systems or intellectual constructions, draw the soul away from itself, forget it. True thought, however, seeks to draw man away from mere temporality and sense objects, from the indigence and nakedness of simple phenomena, and to bring it back to itself, in order that it might see clearly its own being. True thought does not want to draw the soul away

---

[3] Cf. St. Augustine: "Thou madest us for Thyself, and our heart is restless, until it repose in Thee" (*Confessions,* Bk. I).

[4] E.g. communism and socialism.

[5] E.g. Hegelianism and the schools of logical positivism and analytic philosophy.

from itself. The withdrawal of the soul from other things, opposed to its nature — from concrete sensible things and from the passions — is one thing, and quite another is the withdrawal of the soul from itself, and especially to such an extent that it forgets that it is the first value, the source of all other values.

Philosophy, insofar as it is worthy of the name, does not come to draw the soul away from its very being and empty it into other, secondary things, but comes to concentrate the soul into its own core, and this core is its moral, rational, and religious presence. The soul is the eternal center of spirit. This is why it is the true existence. As a spiritual reality, this existence has problems inherent in its being; and these are the problems which we indicated earlier, when we sketched briefly the general image of the soul.

Today's conceptions, being simple cerebrations, ignore the real problems of the soul and above all ignore man as a unique and irreplaceable value, as an intrinsic value, and put in his place other, secondary things, put in his place constructs and mechanical substitutes. They speak of man, not in a concrete manner, but in an altogether abstract way. They speak of rather remote values, of things that man will encounter in the very distant future. They do not speak at all, however, of man as he is in his essence. Whether a certain man, this man here, the concrete and unique man, exists as a point of immortality, as a soul, as a personality — about this the constructs and plans are not at all concerned. But the problem of man as man lies precisely in this: that man himself, the concrete man, each individual, is infinitely interested in his own unique presence and existence; that is, is interested in his irreplaceable value and in his eternity. From this consciousness of immortality come all the great works of the spirit, whereas when this consciousness is absent, it is impossible for great works to be produced. As a result of abstract thought, that is, of constructionist instead of fruitful thought, man has become a schema. All his problems have lost their primal value. Thus the problem of immortality, too, has lost its importance. This happened because the person, as a unique and irreplaceable existence, was put aside by the plans and constructs. Our epoch ignores the personality, or, as Kierkegaard somewhere says, our epoch "kills the person, the concrete monad with personal and unrepeatable presence of spirit, and then teaches the immortality of the general, of the abstract universal," that is, of mankind. Intellectual constructs forget the unique existence of man, his concrete being. Man's essence, however, is that he himself exists as a personal being.

The real man, not the concept of man, lives and moves between the finite and the infinite. On the one hand, he concerns himself with the finite, works with his knowledge and the other basic modes of his soul; and on the other hand, he longs for absolute unity, he is drawn towards it by his religious feeling. The real man, as Plato represented him, lies between the finite and the eternal: the synthesis of these two constitutes the concrete man, the personality. In the personality are combined the finite with the infinite, the striving of the soul to master the world through knowledge with the longing of the soul to withdraw from finite things and taste the infinite. But constructionist, artificial thought, divorces man from this reality of his and disturbs his true relation to his personal being, to the unique and irreplaceable presence of his spirit.

This is something chiefly characteristic of our age. The Christians of the Middle Ages[6] and the philosophers of ancient Greece were preeminently men, that is, they had a very rich inner life, they had personality and lived their personal presence with intensity; or, in contemporary terminology, they were real existences. Today, both thought and technology, both politics and art divorce man from his personal presence, from the value of the person, because all their creations are schemas and do not spring from inner life, from the passion to be. In ancient Greece especially the philosopher not only produced great edifices of the spirit, which were simultaneously works of art, but was himself a work of art. Theory and practice were harmoniously united in him, or at least he had a strong tendency to harmonize them. Only in the post-Classical period of Antiquity did theory begin to be separated from life, spirit

---

[6] Theodorakopoulos has in mind here not only the Christians of the West, but also and especially those of the Hellenic East, of Byzantium. See e.g. pp. 145-146 of the book from which this chapter has been taken, where he speaks of the rise of the Byzantine Empire and the appearance there of figures such as Eusebius, Athanasius the Great, Basil the Great, and Gregory Nazianzen.

from presence, from the existence of man. This separation later became greater and greater, until when Christianity came it found wisdom and knowledge cut off from life, from the presence of man.

Christianity found intellectual life severed from the rest of inner life. The "wisdom of this world," knowledge that is cut off from life, appears from the standpoint of Christianity as something very secondary, because it does not concern itself with the problem "man." To desire to deify such knowledge, which is separated from the soul, which is unrelated to the inner reality of man, would signify that one has already ceased to regard oneself as a personality, as a unique soul and spiritual being. It would mean that one has never been active within, that one has not lived according to one's essence, that is, as a real man. Hence the problem of man is posed by Christianity not according to the wisdom of this world, but in a new way. Now the question is about "the new man" and "the new creation." Christianity turns the life of man inwardly, towards the soul. To exist as a man now means to act not so much outwardly, but rather inwardly. What does this mean? It means to act with the consciousness of an eternal responsibility, because the soul is a point of eternity. This, says Christianity, is something every man can do. Hence to be a man is something altogether different from what it was before. Through their reason, through their naked intellectualism, men had severed themselves before from their soul, from their real root — they lived cerebrally. One must advance very far within the self and experience the presence of its immense power in order to realize how insipid and comical are cerebral constructs, dry intellection. And the more deeply one lives one's unique presence, one's soul, the greater becomes one's consciousness of the emptiness of the intellectual snare which one constructed before. The intellectual snare, logical constructs, even when they have some great idea as their foundation, ignore the essence of that idea and simultaneously ignore the presence of personality. They ignore the indigence and yearning of the soul, that is, the indigence which it feels because it is far from the Immortal and its aspiration to be united with it. But if there is an inviolable principle in the life of man, if there is an inviolable boundary of humanity, it is that one should not forget that he is a person with a yearning for immortality, that he is a soul with an eros for eternity. This is precisely the meaning of the statement that man lies between the finite and the infinite. Life in all its possible intensity is to remember and be concerned about immortality. . . .

The Greek philosophers, especially the great pre-Socratics[7] and the three classical ones: Socrates, Plato, and Aristotle, did not ignore the problem of the soul, did not abolish personality, but saw the soul as an eternal core, as the principle of reason. It is characteristic of ancient Greek philosophy that reason did not separate itself from the soul, from personal existence. Philosophy here is a discipline of the soul, a preparation of man for immortality. Socrates did not advance to an abstract schema nor did he abolish his personality, but saw his being as an eternal point, as something immortal. Plato characterizes philosophy in the *Phaedo* as a meditation on death and a meditation on immortality. He disciplines the intellect, reason, but this discipline of reason is done in direct relation to the soul. Reason is an instrument that helps the soul become conscious of its immortality while still in time. Modern philosophy, on the contrary, especially the systems of the nineteenth century, separated thought from the soul to such an extent that thought became something cut off from the personality, something abstract; and the soul was abandoned, neglected and forgotten.

But the eternal problem which no philosophy can ignore without losing its meaning is that of the soul. Man's infinite concern centers about it; man's yearning is here intensified, because it is here that the purpose of life is found. Man has a depth of immense potentialities; this is the soul. Abstract thought, formal intellectual thought, abandons man's interiority, man's nature, and loses itself in logical acrobatics. What man really is, that he is a personal presence with a yearning for his eternity, this is something which formal discursive thought cannot express. This anxious endeavor is not a movement of the spirit outward, nor is it an attempt to grasp other entities, which are different from spirit, but is a movement inward, where each point of the path is redeemed with absolute self-concentration and solitude. Only thus does man come to

---

7 E.g. Pythagoras, Heraclitus, and Empedocles.

real proximity with himself; only thus does he avoid forgetting himself, that is, his core. Knowledge now becomes fruitful for the discovery of man's essence, whereas before it was fruitful for the discovery, the understanding of things. Thus Socrates reversed the movement of knowledge from outward inward. He put man in the first place and everything else in the second. Since I do not know myself, he remarks, why should I preoccupy myself with other things?

Our epoch is more remote than all others from this Socratic standpoint. That man comes first, that his inner spiritual hypostasis is what should be of infinite concern to each man, this our epoch seems to have entirely forgotten. Today, general schemas and constructs stifle the concrete man, the unique and intrinsic value called man.

Now in order to pay attention to the root of one's self and see one's being as an eternal point, which no general schema can interpret and no theory can vindicate, one requires not only self-concentration, but also faith. Through faith there opens up an infinite concern about the absolute value of personality. Faith has this special characteristic, that it develops an infinite concern about the value of the soul. Faith, however, is a leap beyond mere knowledge, is a self-affirmation of the value called *man* that relates man to eternity.

# FURTHER READING

### ATHANASIOS PSALIDAS (1767-1827)
Alēthēs Eudaimonia, ētoi Basis Pasēs Thrēskeias ("True Happiness, or the Basis of All Religion"), Vienna, 1791. (The text is accompanied by a Latin translation made by the author, and hence the book is also known by its Latin title: *Vera Felicitas, sive Fundamentum Omnis Religionis.*)

### KONSTANTINOS KOUMAS (1777-1836)
Krēpis Philosophias ("Foundations of Philosophy"), Vienna, 1818, Chs. 4 and 5.

### NEOPHYTOS DOUKAS (1760-1845)
Tetraktys, ētoi Rhētorikē, Logikē, Metaphysikē, kai Ēthikē ("Tetraktys, or Rhetoric, Logic, Metaphysics, and Ethics"), Aegina, 1834, pp. 165-173.

### NEOPHYTOS VAMVAS (1770-1855)
Stoicheia Philosophias ("Elements of Philosophy"), Athens, 1838, pp. 292-295.

### THEOPHILOS KAIRIS (1784-1853)
Philosophika ("Philosophical Studies"), 2nd ed., Athens, 1910, pp. 122-126.

### ELISAIOS GIANIDIS (1865-1941)
To Megalo Problēma: Dokimio kritikēs tou hylismou ("The Great Problem: A critical essay on materialism"), Athens, 1925.

NICHOLAS LOUVARIS (1887-1961)
*Metaxy Duo Kosmōn* ("Between Two Worlds"), Athens, 1949, esp. pp. 25-27, 31, 141-142, 342-343.
*Symposion Hosiōn* ("Symposium of Holy Men"), Vol. I, Athens, 1962, pp. 104-109.

IOEL GIANNAKOPOULOS (1901-1966)
*Hyparchei Psychē?* ("Is there a Soul?"), Kalamai, 1951.

A considerably longer bibliography could be given. I have simply listed some of the more noteworthy authors who have argued for the immateriality and immortality of the soul, and the works in which they deal with this subject, or deal with it most effectively. All these men were prominent educators, and some of them — Psalidas, Koumas, and Doukas — have been named Educators of the Nation. These three writers, as well as Kairis and Louvaris, are among the more significant modern Greek philosophers. Gianidis was a scientist; he was trained in chemistry and mathematics, and taught these subjects. Giannakopoulos was a theologian and religious philosopher.

In his above mentioned book, PSALIDAS argues that man's natural and supernatural happiness requires the certain and indubitable knowledge of four principles: the Existence of God, the Freedom of Man, the Immortality of the Soul, and Retribution After Death; that we can know these principles neither through philosophy, nor through science; but that we know them through Divine revelation, with a certainty which philosophical and empirical scientific knowledge do not possess. KOUMAS follows mainly Kant's line of reasoning, as developed in the *Critique of Practical Reason,* arguing that the existence of God, the freedom of the will, and the immortality of the soul are postulates of practical reason, required by objective morality, whose aim is the attainment of the Summum Bonum—Virtue and Happiness proportioned to it. But unlike Kant, who rejects the traditional philosophical arguments for the existence of God, Koumas affirms their validity. Further, he affirms the Christian doctrine of the resurrection. The approach of DOUKAS and KAIRIS to the question of the soul is essentially the same as that of Benjamin, although they bring out some new points. Their discussion of the subject is, however, rather brief. VAMVAS argues for the incorporeality and immortality of the psyche from religious experience. His treatment, too, is brief. GIANIDIS approaches the question from the side of the natural sciences. He shows the fallacy of the claim that modern scientific advances have disproved the existence of God and the immortality of the soul. LOUVARIS seeks to defend the spiritual nature and immortality of the soul by showing the inadequacy of materialism, naturalism, and pantheism as world views, and the superiority of the world view of personalistic idealism or theism, especially Christianity. Finally, GIANNAKOPOULOS resolves the problem of the psyche by utilizing the data of physiology, psychology, and psychoanalysis, as well as the teachings of Christ, of "the elementary philosophy of life" and of ethics.

C. C.

# INDEX

actuality, 94-5
Ampere, 38, 47
Anarcharsis, 28
animals, 33-4, 39, 78, 81, 94
annihilation, 22, 36
Archimedes, 27
Aristippus, 85
Aristotle, 7, 8, 16, 17, 33, 38 47, 52, 77, 82, 85, 94, 104
Aristoxenus, 18
Athanasius, St., 9, 62, 83, 102
attention, 35, 49, 53
Augustine, St., 100

Bacon, 47
Basil, St., 102
Benjamin of Lesvos, 3, 10, 15-28, 107
Bergson, 20, 35, 53
body, 7, 9, 10, 18, 19, 20, 22, 33, 34, 36, 50, 51, 53, 54, 62-3, 80, 92
brain, 46, 47, 49, 83
Buchner, 45, 46, 47
Burch, George B., 4
Byzantines, 8-9, 10, 77, 102
Byzantium, 8, 9, 102

Cabanis, 83
Cauchy, 38

Chevreul, 47
Christ, 9, 54, 108
Christ, 9, 54, 108
Christianity, 8-9, 10, 44, 47, 76, 90, 100, 102-3, 108
Chrysostom, John, St., 25
Clement of Alexandria, 8-9, 58
Confucius, 28
conscience, 24, 73-5, 98
consciousness, 9, 10, 18, 20, 23, 35, 48, 52, 53, 93, 94, 96
Copernicus, 38
Cousin, Victor, 52

Davy, 47
Descartes, 27, 38
Diagoras, 85
Dostoievsky, 34
Doukas, Neophytos, 106, 107
Dumas, 38

education, 94
Emerson, 34, 63-4, 67
emotions, 50-1
Empedocles, 8, 104
Epicureans, 64, 85
Epicurus, 18
ethics, 15, 32, 65-6, 83-6, 95-8
Eusebius, 102

faith, 10, 11, 25, 32, 54, 60, 105
Faraday, 47

# Index

feeling, 18, 20, 24, 94, 95, 98
Fiske, John, 25, 48
Franklin, 54
freedom, 20-22, 24
  cognitive, 49, 64, 97
  of the will, 49-50, 64, 107
Fresnel, 38

Galen, 18
Galileo, 38
Gianidis, Elisaios, 107, 108
Giannakopoulos, Ioel, 106, 108
God, 9, 10, 21-8, 33, 36, 37, 38, 44, 48, 58, 59, 60, 65-7, 72, 78, 80-1, 98-100, 107, 108
Gregory Nazianzen, St., 102
Gregory of Nyssa, St., 9

Haller, 47
happiness, 23, 24, 26, 65-8, 107
Hegelianism, 100
Hegesias, 85
Heraclitus, 8, 104
Herschel, 15
Hocking, William E., 50
Hugo, 53-4
Humbolt, 47
Huxley, Thomas H., 47, 48

imagination, 35, 50, 53, 95-7
immortality, 3, 7, 8, 9, 11, 22-28, 33, 36-7, 44, 53-4, 59-86, 95, 100-5, 107-8
intellect, 17, 34, 39, 53, 61, 69, 104
introspection, 10, 32, 34

James, William, 68
Jaspers, Karl, 54, 63-4

Kairis, Theophilos, 106, 107
Kant, 107
Kepler, 38
Kierkegaard, 101-2
knowledge, 91-2, 95-6, 98, 102, 105

eros for, 81-3
innate, 24, 25, 26, 68, 75
Koumas, Konstantinos, 106, 107
Krafft-Ebing, 46, 49

Laplace, 38
Leibniz, 38, 52, 54
Liebig, 38
life, 39, 45
Locke, 16
Louvaris, Nicholas, 107

Maine de Biran, 54
man, 7, 9, 20, 24, 34, 45, 61, 70, 77, 78, 97, 101-5
Mann, Thomas, 34
materialism, 9, 10, 19, 32, 38, 44, 45-50, 80, 85, 108
matter, 20, 26, 34, 35, 39, 61, 72
Maximus the Confessor, 9
Mayer, 38
memory, 18, 19, 35
metaphysics, 10, 15, 32, 39

naturalism, 9, 108
Naville, Ernest, 38
Nectarios, St., 3, 11, 55-86
Newton, 27, 28, 38

Orpheus, 28

pantheism, 108
Pasteur, 38
Paul, St., 23, 75
perception, 35, 39
personality, 50, 51, 52, 53, 96, 97, 99, 101-2, 104-5
philosophy, 39-40, 44, 58, 71, 72, 101, 104, 107
  ancient Greek, 7-10, 44, 52, 58, 102, 104
  Byzantine, 8-9
  modern European, 10, 33, 44, 52, 104
physiology, 34, 39, 108

# Index

Plato, 7, 9, 16, 17, 23, 27, 34, 37, 38, 48, 58, 62, 64-5, 85, 90, 92, 95, 98, 102, 104
Plutarch, 85
positivism, 9, 38, 39, 100
potentiality, 94-5, 104
Pratt, James B., 20
preexistence, 9
Psalidas, Athanasios, 106, 107
psychology, 39, 92, 108
Pythagoras, 8, 27, 104

reason, 8, 9, 10, 26, 32, 36, 60, 62, 103, 104
reincarnation, 9
religion, 10, 44, 77, 78-80, 98-9
responsibility, 49, 95, 96, 103
resurrection, 9, 107
revelation, 59, 60, 69, 75-6, 107

science, 10, 15, 19-20, 26-7, 32, 37-40, 44, 48, 49, 107, 108
Scripture, 9, 33, 59, 77-8
self-concentration, 104-5
self-knowledge, 17
sensations, 17, 18, 39, 92
Sinnott, Edmund W., 39
Skaltsounis, Ioannis, 3, 11, 41-54
Socrates, 7, 28, 38, 53, 85, 90, 104, 105
soul,
    a creature, 10, 23
    dignity of, 7, 8, 9, 37, 60, 97
    immaterial, 9, 10, 20, 33, 35, 51, 53, 64, 65, 92, 107, 108
    immortal, *see* immortality
    indivisible, 10, 34
    rational, 9, 10, 20, 36-7, 100, 101
    self-active, 9, 10, 20, 35, 62, 93-4, 98
    self-conscious, 9, 10, 35, 48, 51, 62, 64, 95
    simple, 9, 10, 20, 22, 64, 65
    a substance, 9, 10, 19, 93, 95
    a unity, 34, 35, 36, 51, 92, 93, 94, 99, 100
Soury, Jules, 45, 46, 47
Sperry, Roger, 49
spirit, 20, 23, 96, 97, 101
substance, 20

Theodorakopoulos, I. N., 3, 11, 87-105

Vamvas, Neophytos, 106, 108
Vrailas-Armenis, Petros, 3, 10-11, 29-40

Whitehead, Alfred N., 20, 38, 39-40
will, 18, 49, 51, 95, 97